INDIANAPOLIS
GRAVEROBBING

INDIANAPOLIS GRAVEROBBING

A SYNDICATE OF DEATH

CHRIS FLOOK

THE
History
PRESS

Published by The History Press
Charleston, SC
www.historypress.com

First published 2023

Manufactured in the United States

ISBN 9781467151092

Library of Congress Control Number: 2023934830

Notice: The information in this book is true and complete to the best of our knowledge. It is offered without guarantee on the part of the author or The History Press. The author and The History Press disclaim all liability in connection with the use of this book.

Dedicated to Kourtney McCauliff, my wonderful partner in crime.
She wouldn't help me dig up a body, but she would definitely help me hide one.
Love you!

CONTENTS

ACKNOWLEDGEMENTS

I 'm grateful to be living in a time with so much information readily available at my fingertips from home. This book exists only because of the archives, repositories, libraries and museums that offer easy online access to their collections for exploration. Many thanks to the Hoosier State Chronicles, Library of Congress, Wellcome Collection, Ancestry. com, Newspapers.com, the Indiana Historical Society, the Indianapolis-Marion County Public Library, the Indiana State Library, Archive.org and WikiCommons. I started research for this book and wrote the first half when everything was shut down during the COVID-19 pandemic. I deeply appreciate these organizations' online services, which made work possible in such a time.

I'm also grateful to the Indiana Archives and Records Administration and the Indiana State Library for permission to use several high-resolution photos. Vicki Casteel, the director of patron and outreach services at the IARA, and Lauren Patton, rare books and manuscripts librarian at the State Library, were both instrumental in getting what I needed. Thank you both!

Finally, I'd like to recognize my mother, Kathleen Flook. Her resolute encouragement over the years has nurtured me to become a disciplined writer. Mom's review of an early draft of this book also caught more than a few grammatical errors. As a retired high school English teacher, she's been instrumental in cultivating good grammar and simplicity in my writing for decades! I owe (and love) her a lot.

A SHOOT-OUT
IN DESOTO, INDIANA

After the discovery of natural gas near Eaton in 1886, communities across east-central Indiana began a rapid process of extraction that became known as the "Indiana gas and oil boom." Thousands flocked to the gas-belt industrial centers of Muncie, Anderson, Kokomo and Marion for factory jobs. Oil had also become commercially exploitable in the region by 1904. Wells dotted the landscape near the small agricultural rail towns in eastern Delaware County.

In the late evening hours of Monday, November 28, 1904, an oil worker on his way to a nightshift walked past the Union Church Cemetery in DeSoto. A small farming village with a busy rail depot at the time, DeSoto is situated about seven miles northeast of Muncie on what was then the Lake Erie and Western Railroad.

Most nights, the cemetery was dark and inhabited perhaps only by spirits of farmers laid to rest in the village's only burial ground. However, on this particular night, the roughneck noticed four men rapidly digging, their shovels and pickaxes tearing away the earth at what appeared to be a freshly dug grave. Sensing mischief, he rode swiftly to a nearby farm in alarm.[1]

The farmer gathered a posse of armed villagers and went directly to the cemetery. The graverobbers fled as they approached, leaving evidence of their work behind. Sod and earth covered the ground around the recently dug grave of Reverend John Alexander Pittenger. The farmers had disrupted the graverobbing, and for the moment, the good reverend remained safely buried.

Frederik Ruysch's *Thesaurus Anatomicus* (1701). *Wellcome Collection.*

On the following night, Pittenger's brothers, Marion and Nichols, stood guard over their sibling's grave, waiting for the return of the body snatchers. At about 9:00 p.m., the brothers spotted four lights in the distance approaching the cemetery. The Pittengers rounded up another posse of villagers, who gathered once again to fend off the graverobbers.[2] Whatever the lights were, they disappeared to whence they came.

The brothers maintained a nightly vigil for a week at a nearby abandoned farmhouse, which provided a commanding view of Union Chapel. In the small hours of December 6, the brothers spotted two buggies quietly lumbering down the road. Four men got out at the cemetery's gates and began digging again at the reverend's grave. The Pittengers opened fire on the body snatchers, who returned their volleys in what ended up becoming an early morning gun battle. Louisville's *Courier-Journal* reported that "the brothers fired upon them and the ghouls returned the shots, taking refuge behind the tombstones and gradually [worked] their way back to the buggies"[3] and quickly disembarked down the road. The two other graverobbers became separated in the melee and scaled "the cemetery fence, ran down the highway, where they were joined by the men who had succeeded in reaching the buggies."[4]

The Pittengers thought that they fired about twenty shots. As the sun rose, blood was discovered on a grave marker. A bullet had hit its mark.

As we shall see, graverobbing attempts such as this were common in central Indiana around 1900. Body snatchers had carried out such ghastly work across the Hoosier state for decades. Unlike the tomb raiders of yore, who searched for treasures long buried with forgotten kings, graverobbers in the late nineteenth and early twentieth centuries went after fresh corpses—bodies highly valued by the state's medical colleges as cadavers. In DeSoto's Union Church Cemetery and in several other nearby burial plots, it was determined that the robbers had dug into numerous graves in the fall of 1904.[5]

For several nights, armed residents stood watch over the cemetery, although the ghouls were never seen again. The *Huntington Weekly Herald* reported

A London hospital "dissecting room" around 1900. *Wellcome Collection.*

that DeSotoan farmers intended to "shoot to kill any suspicious-appearing person who enters the ground after nightfall."[6] Revered Pittenger, to this day, remains at rest, courtesy of villagers armed with pistols and shotguns. Yet, as we shall see, thousands of other Hoosiers do not.

INTRODUCTION

The story you're about to read is a grisly tale of graverobbing in turn-of-the-century Indianapolis. In September 1902, city police detectives uncovered a body snatching ring operating out of Marion County. The previous summer, ghoulish graverobbers had plundered cemeteries across central Indiana, stealing the remains of the recently deceased and selling their corpses to Indianapolis medical schools for dissection. A few of those arrested turned state's evidence and provided investigators with macabre details about the graverobbers' activities. Local press sensationalized accounts, sharing headlines with newspapers across the United States. The subsequent trials captured the public's attention well into 1903.

This story is well known today in Indianapolis. In recent years, several writers and historians have recounted the tale for modern audiences. In 2015, Stephen J. Taylor wrote the article "Rufus Cantrell, Intruder in the Dust" for HistoricIndianapolis.com.[7] One year later, Dawn Mitchell penned "The Business of Body Snatching in Indianapolis" for the *Indy Star*.[8] David Heighway, the erudite Hamilton County historian, has written and spoken on the subject several times.[9] Then, in 2020, Lindsey Beckley wrote the article "'King of the Ghouls': Rufus Cantrell & Grave-Robbing in Indianapolis" for the Indiana Historical Bureau,[10] and the *Talking Hoosier History* podcast released an episode titled "Rufus Cantrell: King of the Ghouls."[11]

I first learned of this story many years ago when reading Keven McQueen's wonderful *Forgotten Tales of Indiana*. I was reminded of it in 2017 after coming

Busy Meridian Street in the early 1900s. *Library of Congress.*

across a 1904 *Muncie Morning Star* newspaper article about the graverobbing attempt in DeSoto, the subject of the prologue. Like all good stories, this one prompted lots of follow-up questions. The subsequent research led me back to the Indianapolis graverobbers and down a rabbit hole of ghastly cemetery exploits, murder, political intrigue, conspiracy and racism.

I hope this book contributes to a better understanding of the story by providing a detailed, week-by-week accounting of it. The greater arc is interesting enough, but the particulars are far more fascinating and, frankly, downright bizarre. I also found tons of photos in the public domain that will, ideally, flesh out the characters as the real human beings they were. However, my main motivation in writing the book was simply that I wanted to tell the true-crime graverobbing story of Rufus Cantrell, Wade West and Dr. Joseph Alexander. I find the story totally engrossing, and I hope you will too.

Readers should note that most of my sources are local newspapers, the *Indianapolis Journal* and *Indianapolis News* especially. I found the newspaper reports to be, in the main, an honest description of events, but some of the particulars weren't always accurate or turned out to be downright fabrications. The sensational nature of the story also pushed some reporters to run with rumors that were misleading. I know we like to think of our own era as one of fake news, but it pales in comparison to the yellow journalism of the early 1900s. Throughout the book, I noted where I found reports inaccurate and which "facts" were actually rumors. Some of the dialogue in these articles also seemed partially contrived and, in some cases, even totally made up. There's unfortunately no other source to verify the statements. All of this is simply to say: newspapers of the era should be read with a critical eye. I've provided comprehensive notes throughout, citing the specific articles I sourced information from. Readers are invited to their own interpretations based on these references.

Despite the limitations, the newspapers make it clear that racism played a decisive role in how the participants were adjudicated. All but one of the white body snatchers involved in the ring got away with their crimes, a fate not shared by their counterparts of color. The Black graverobbers received a disproportionate amount of blame and punishment for a criminal conspiracy created, managed and maintained by white doctors at some of the city's medical schools. These anatomists employed or contracted with mostly white

The corner of Delaware and Virginia in the early 1900s. *From* The Journal Handbook of Indianapolis, *Indianapolis–Marion County Public Library.*

17

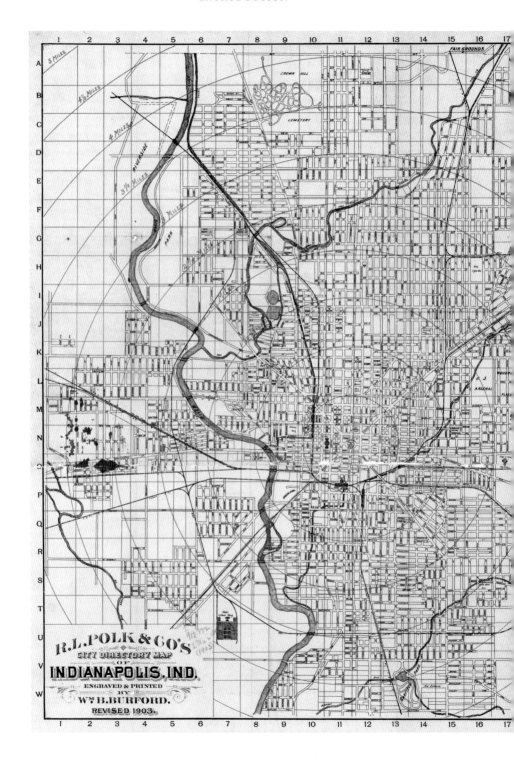

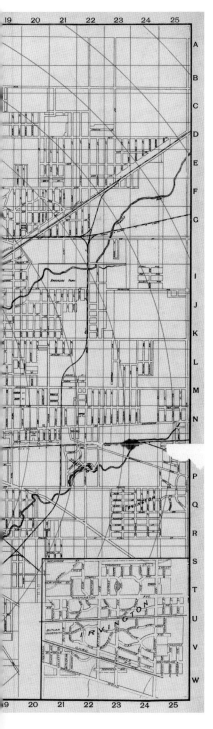

body snatchers across central Indiana, the vast majority of whom never faced any legal consequences. Readers should be aware that the ugly specter of American racism appears throughout the story.

You should also note my approach to research, time and plot. I knew the story's general arc prior to writing the book but didn't know any details until I actually sat down and read the archived newspapers. This book was written and arranged chronologically, with the story unfolding as I found it and as Hoosiers would have read it in 1902 and 1903.

Finally, I used the words *ghoul, body snatcher, graverobber* and *resurrectionist* interchangeably to describe all participants involved in stealing bodies for medical schools. The word *ghoul* comes from the Arabic word *ghūl*, a name for a corpse-eating demon that haunts cemeteries in pre-Islamic folklore. Such a word is a fitting description for the historical characters you're about to meet. So, as you find the sun sinking low, nestle into your most comfortable chair, grab a favorite beverage and start in on this grim tale of Hoosier ghouls.

City directory map of Indy from 1903. Image from the *Map Collection, Indiana Division, Indiana State Library.*

CHAPTER 1

WHERE IS GLENDORA GATES?

I n the late evening of Wednesday, September 17, 1902, Julia Middleton returned to her home at 24 Gladstone Avenue after attending a prayer service in Irvington. She discovered a note that someone had slipped underneath her front door. The missive stopped her cold in the entryway. Although history does not record the exact message, the *Indianapolis Journal* reported that "the note stated that the body of her daughter had been removed from its resting place in the graveyard and could be found at Central College. No name was signed to the note."[12] Julia's daughter Stella had died earlier that summer at sixteen, probably from tuberculosis, and was laid to rest at Anderson Cemetery on Tenth Street.

Naturally alarmed, Middleton consulted with relatives, who advised her to inquire at the Central College of Physicians and Surgeons, just as the note instructed. The Middleton family received a search warrant from William Nickerson, a Marion County Center Township justice of the peace. The search party then proceeded to Central College on South Street with a court-appointed constable.[13] There they discovered Stella's corpse "lying on a cooling board with several other bodies."[14]

Cadavers were a common sight at Central College, as the school trained budding physicians, but Stella's body hadn't been donated. Her understandably distraught mother refused to leave the room until an undertaker arrived. After collecting Stella's remains, morticians immediately reburied them, this time with additional boards placed over the coffin.

A typical medial college dissecting room. *Photo by J.B. Walters (1897), "The Dissection Room, Medical School, Newcastle upon Tyne," Wellcome Collection, attribution 4.0 International (CC BY 4.0).*

The same night Mrs. Middleton received her note, a strange man paid a visit to Wesley Gates in Irvington. Gates had lost his daughter Glendora that summer to tuberculosis as well, and just like Stella, she was interred at Anderson Cemetery. The mysterious informant told Gates that "someone in a carriage would like to talk to him. Gates went out to the coach and from behind the curtains a muffled voice told him that a plan had been made to steal the body of his daughter from the Anderson graveyard."[15]

If he wanted her body back, Gates could find it at Central College. The carriage then drove off into the night. Gates, suspicious but not convinced, rallied some friends and proceeded to the Anderson Cemetery, where he dug at the head of his daughter's grave. Upon reaching the coffin, he found nothing amiss and replaced the dirt as he found it. Gates told police investigators that even though his daughter's grave appeared unmolested, several nearby plots had been recently disturbed.

The related events raised the suspicions of the Indianapolis Police Department. Central College's Dean Maxwell admitted to detectives that "he knew of the body of the Middleton girl being brought to the college, but he did not know from where it came." The college had made arrangements to retrieve cadavers with its demonstrator, Dr. Joseph Alexander, who provided "the college with bodies for dissecting purposes." Central College, according to Maxwell, had nothing to do with the theft of Stella Middleton's body, but he did note that she "was brought to the college by a colored man, and he thought the colored man was paid by Dr. Alexander."[16]

Medical colleges behaving badly with cadavers wasn't a new phenomenon in the Circle City, but Indianapolis police captain Samuel Gerber sensed a larger conspiracy. He assigned Detective Adolph Asch and patrolman Chauncey Manning to investigate. Asch, a Jewish immigrant from France, was a veteran IPD detective, while Manning was a master interrogator.

The following Friday, an anonymous informant placed a call to Manson Neidlinger of New Augusta. Neidlinger recognized the voice on the line, for the same man had phoned earlier in the week with an important message and requested to meet in person. During the first call, Neidlinger inquired as to the informant's identity. The voice replied, "It will do you no good to know who I am. I am trying to be a friend of yours. The information I want to give you, you will consider very important. I will be at your house within two hours."[17] The caller never showed, and Neidlinger went to bed thinking it was a prank.

Early twentieth-century IPD wagon. *Library of Congress.*

DETECTIVES WHO TRACED THE GRAVE ROBBERS.

ADOLPH ASCH.   CHAUNCEY MANNING

Detective Asch and patrolman Manning, from the *Indianapolis News*, September 29, 1902. *Hoosier State Chronicles.*

When the mysterious informant called the second time on Friday, he told Neidlinger that he wasn't able to make it to New Augusta but that "if he went to the Pleasant Hill Graveyard and opened the grave of his wife he would find the body missing."[18] He added that her corpse could be found at Central College. If the now overwrought Neidlinger acted quickly, he could retrieve it. The informant then asked for a reward and hung up.

Manson Neidlinger laid awake the whole night worrying about the macabre message. Rosielee Neidlinger had died young on July 17 from tuberculosis and was indeed buried at New Augusta's Pleasant Hill Cemetery. The next morning, Neidlinger met up with his brother Frank to open Rose's grave. The Neidlingers were accompanied by Joseph Cropper, a New Augusta constable, and brothers Clark and Alfred Frank to carry out the grisly task:

> *The men went to the graveyard shortly after daybreak. They found the grave in perfect condition, and were at first inclined not to open it. Nothing about*

the grave showed signs it had been tampered with. Neidlinger, however, would not rest until he had seen the inside of the coffin. The grave was opened and the body found missing.[19]

Neidlinger and his fellow diggers proceeded to the office of James Collins, deputy prosecutor for the Indianapolis Police Court. Collins issued a warrant and tasked Constable Cropper to carry out a search of Central College. Neidlinger also asked for police to accompany them, a request granted by two bicycle patrolmen.

The search party found the college closed, without anyone to allow entry. The Middleton and Gates stories were becoming sensationalized in the press, and several reporters had gathered around the entrance hoping to catch new info from those coming and going. Wishing to keep their task secret, Neidlinger's searchers opted to leave and return later in the evening.

The reporters had all left by 8:00 p.m. As night fell, two interns let Neidlinger's party in through the back of Central College. The searchers discovered a woman's cadaver "lying on a dissecting table,"[20] but it wasn't Rose. The internists then rolled out a large barrel and removed a pickled female corpse. This seems ghastly today, but it was a common practice at the time for college demonstrators to preserve cadavers in brine until dissection. But this was no dissecting cadaver—it was a pickled Rose Neidlinger.

Manson recognized his wife immediately "by a scar in the middle of the forehead."[21] Quite understandably, he became extremely upset and "more perturbed the longer he remained at the college."[22] The body was removed by Flanner and Buchanan Funeral Home and prepared for burial a second time at Pleasant Hill Cemetery.

Dr. Joseph Alexander again appeared to be at the center of the controversy, although he expressed total ignorance when questioned. "He felt hurt at the turn of affairs within the past week. He had not known from whence the body came or to whom it belonged."[23] He told reporters that "he was sorry that the body was stolen," adding the lie, "the public institutions furnish plenty of cadavers for dissecting purposes."[24]

The discovery of Middleton and Neidlinger bodies at Central College created a minor scandal in Indianapolis. Although the reports were, at first, overshadowed in Indy by a visit from President Roosevelt, the story gained traction as the weeks progressed. The scale of the operation alarmed many but didn't really surprise anyone. Resurrectionists had operated in Indianapolis for years with little interference. Body snatching was abhorred by the public, but the practice was not unknown.

Indianapolis police detectives Asch and Manning continued to investigate the case but received a break at week's end that led to several arrests. The first tip came from Gus Habich, a gunsmith with a retail store at 108 West Market Street. Habich filed a writ of replevin (a legal remedy to recover stolen property) for several guns. He had sold revolvers to a man named Rufus Cantrell on credit. He told police that Dr. J.C. Alexander of Central College and Dr. Frank Wright, secretary and treasurer of the Electic Medical College, agreed to pay for the weapons, although Habich never received money.

Joseph Alexander from the *Indianapolis News*, September 29, 1902. *Hoosier State Chronicles*.

His clerk, A.E. McKee, also reported to police that Cantrell was in the store recently boasting about his graverobbing prowess. McKee had even overheard a telephone conversation between the ghoul and Dr. Alexander about the price of "resurrected" bodies. Cantrell threatened McKee when the clerk asked for his guns back.[25]

The detectives received another clue from Emil Mantell, a pawnbroker at 205 West Washington Street. Mantell had loaned "$28 on four shotguns presented by a negro."[26] The pawnbroker supposedly became suspicious of the individual pawning the guns and phoned his attorney, Taylor Groninger, about what to do.[27] Groninger, a former deputy prosecutor, asked to whom the loan was made, and Mantel gave the name Rufus Cantrell. The lawyer was "familiar with the name of Rufus Cantrell, and knew his reputation as a ghoul,"[28] someone paid by medical colleges to illegally procure fresh cadavers for dissection. As with Habich's story, cops passed all information on to Asch and Manning.

The detectives now had enough evidence to make arrests. Sam Martin, Garfield Buckner, William Jones, Isom Donnel, Sol Grady, Walter Daniels and Rufus Cantrell were arrested late in the evening on Sunday, September 28, and held on charges of graverobbing. The press identified these men as African American.[29] The police also issued arrest warrants for Dr. J.C. Alexander, Dr. J.C. Wilson and Central College's janitor George Haymaker, all of whom were white. Within hours of their arrest, all three Central College employees posted bail, but the seven Black resurrectionists did not and remained behind bars.[30]

Rufus Cantrell, the nominal head of the crew of graverobbers, turned state's evidence and immediately divulged details about the ring to investigators. Cantrell was unreserved during questioning, requesting leniency in exchange for information. He told detectives almost whatever they wanted to know and, over the course of the next few months, a whole lot more than what they asked for. Rufus disclosed that at least one hundred graves had "been robbed by the ghouls during the last three months."[31] His team carried out their task "armed with shotguns and equipped with horses and wagons with which to do their work. The bodies were sold to different colleges which opened their winter terms within the last week."[32]

Cantrell's crew had carried out the ghoulish work all over Marion County that summer with reckless abandon. At Mount Jackson Cemetery, "we pretty near cleared the place out," Cantrell supposedly said. "I don't believe we missed any body that has been planted there since July."[33] Cantrell and

GRAVE ROBBING GANG AND MEDICAL COLLEGE JANITOR.
[From a Photograph Taken by The News at the Police Station.]

READING FROM LEFT TO RIGHT: GARFIELD BUCKNER, SAM MARTIN, GEORGE HAYMAKER (the janitor), WALTER DAN-IELS, RUFUS CANTRELL, SOL GRADY, ISOM DONNELL, BILL JONES.

Cantrell's graverobbers from the *Indianapolis News*, September 29, 1902. *Hoosier State Chronicles.*

New York Herald photo of Mount Jackson Cemetery, August 16, 1903. *Library of Congress.*

his crew were paid well by college anatomists, who needed the fresh corpses for instruction. Rufus told detectives that he had made $420 in the months from July through September, a substantial sum in 1902. The crew worked "in a systematic manner, and that this is the reason more graves were not discovered to have been robbed."[34]

The resurrectionists dug into the center of the graves and removed the bodies carefully so as to not disturb the surroundings. Everything was put back as it was before, save for the body. Any jewelry was stolen, and the corpses were bagged and transported to a medical college paying for the cadavers. Cantrell's ghouls targeted fresh graves, as digging into already disturbed earth would raise little suspicion. Plus, the colleges needed fresh cadavers for accurate anatomical instruction. The entire operation was carried out in total darkness, except for a single match that was used to illuminate the grave as the body was pulled out.

After their arrests, Cantrell and the six other resurrectionists surely realized that they would receive a disproportionate amount of punishment because of their skin color. Racism in the criminal justice system was as rampant then as it is now. The graverobbers provided information to detectives perhaps out of spite for their white employers, who could leverage ample support from a lenient criminal justice system, or maybe they were just getting bad legal advice.

Regardless of their motivations, everyone pointed to Dr. Joseph C. Alexander as the primary purchaser of bodies at Central College. The ghouls often collected payment from the doctor at his office in the Newton Claypool Building. Cantrell told police that Dr. Alexander would, on occasion, even accompany the body snatchers to do their work. He also went on scouting missions with Cantrell to survey cemeteries to plunder.

Rufus stole corpses from graveyards all over Marion County, including "Pleasant Hill cemetery, near Traders Point; Jones Chapel cemetery, in the same neighborhood, and the German-Catholic cemetery, south of the city."[35] The graverobbers also worked in Ebenezer Cemetery and Mount Jackson Cemetery, which "had suffered from their depredations to a greater extent than any other place, because of the easy access from the city and because the ghouls were not disturbed."[36] When questioned about robbing graves at the city's preeminent cemetery, Crown Hill, Cantrell responded, "You'll have to see certain colored undertakers in this city for that."[37] He added, "You know there are watchmen in that place, and they make the rounds every two hours. It only takes twenty-five minutes to lift a stiff and replace the grave in the same condition."[38] Cantrell also admitted to stealing a corpse from the cemetery at Central Hospital for the Insane after "Dr. Alexander told me to go ahead and lift a certain body, as it has been paid for. We went into the place and got the body without trouble. There was no one about the place."[39]

The ghoul told reporters that most smaller cemeteries in the city had been ransacked and that his crew was but one of many operating in central Indiana, including a gang of "white men who operate all over the State."[40] Cantrell was labeled as the King of the Ghouls, but in all actuality, he was one of several successful body snatching kingpins in central Indiana.

Once "resurrected," the corpses were hauled by the ghouls to any one of several medical colleges in Indiana, most of which were in Indianapolis. The *Indianapolis News* reported how the corpses were exchanged:

> *When the bodies are taken to the college in the wagon used by the ghouls, the horses are driven into a small alleyway in the rear of the building. An electric button on the outside of the door is pushed a certain number of times and a woman, said to be the wife of the janitor, appears at one of the windows above. The signal "Rufus" is given by the ghouls, and the*

Central State Hospital around 1902. *From* The Journal Handbook of Indianapolis, *Indianapolis–Marion County Public Library.*

woman disappears. A moment later the door is noiselessly opened and the bodies are carried inside.[41]

Dr. Alexander denied involvement in any illegal activities. When a reporter asked him about his arrest, Alexander replied, "Aside from the unpleasant notoriety that this affair is occasioning, I am not at all worried. The thing will come out all right, and I will be cleared of the charges against me."[42] After learning about Cantrell's confession, Alexander added a careful response: "The only thing that keeps this from being a good story is that it is a lie from beginning to end. His statement that I accompanied the robbers on their trips is utterly false, as is his statement that I guaranteed the payment for guns bought by the gang."[43] He ended, "Cantrell's whole confession is a lie. I stand by my statement of last week—that I do not know where the bodies I bought for the college came from."[44]

Cantrell, on the other hand, didn't show the least bit of remorse, or so the papers told readers. Though unseemly and immoral, graverobbing was a lucrative trade for those willing and able. In many cities in the United States, body snatching was even a rite of passage for doctors in training. Plus, the demand for fresh cadavers was coming from professional men with social capital who, on occasion, participated in graverobbing themselves.

In addition to orchestrating it all, the anatomists at the medical colleges paid the resurrectionists well.

"I'm not ashamed of what I have done and would probably do it all over again," Cantrell told reporters. "Grave-robbing is a legitimate business and it's no disgrace to be in it. The best physicians in the city have told me and the others in the gang that the laws were such in this State that we could not be arrested." As in most cities across the United States, Black men were often denied well-paying jobs and barred from careers dominated by white people. Body snatching, morality aside, paid well and didn't discriminate.

Cantrell also admitted to stealing the body of Glendora Gates. His confession of the process by which he stole corpses, by digging in the middle of the grave and opening the coffin at the center, explains why Wesley Gates had assumed that his daughter remained safely entombed, for he had opened the grave at the undisturbed head end. After Cantrell's admission, Glendora's brother-in-law, D.S. Bowman, dug into her grave once again, this time at the center. He found a broken lid and an empty coffin.

Where was Glendora Gates?

CHAPTER 2
HOOSIER GHOULS

Although Cantrell's confessions about the graverobbing ring became a sensational story in the press, it didn't really surprise anyone. Hoosier ghouls had operated for years in Indiana, and despite laws written to provide the state's nascent medical colleges with a legal means to obtain cadavers, there were never enough bodies. In the nineteenth century, body snatching was just how many colleges obtained sufficient numbers of cadavers to train their ever-increasing enrollment of students.

Throughout most of the United States, especially in the early and mid-nineteenth century, anatomists legally obtained cadavers from the bodies of executed criminals. Yet not enough people were put to death, leaving a demand for corpses without a sufficient supply.[45] As such, according to the historian Michael Sappol, "the only remaining source of cadavers was the grave."[46]

As the American medical profession advanced from crude apprenticeships to anatomical instruction, medical education became "an active/interactive demonstration rather than the usual didactic experience offered by the medical training programs. Human cadavers were necessary for classroom dissection," according to Suzanne Shultz, another authoritative historian of the subject.[47] Without a sufficient supply of corpses, anatomists and students snatched bodies to fill the gap or hired others to do the dirty work.

When flagrant thefts were discovered by the public, the result was often a violent backlash. Sappol in *A Traffic of Dead Bodies* wrote:

Between 1785–1855, there were at least seventeen anatomy riots in the United States, and numerous minor incidents, affecting nearly every institution of medical learning. Outraged citizens reclaimed their dead, mobbed body snatchers and anatomists, stormed medical colleges, rioted in the streets against militia and police.[48]

New Yorkers in 1788 rampaged against the students and doctors at New York Hospital. Anatomists had raided paupers' graves around the city to obtain cadavers, targeting African American cemeteries. When discovered, a mob two thousand strong ransacked the hospital and destroyed the corpses. The governor even had to call in the militia to quell the uprising.

The most famous case occurred in Scotland in 1828, when William Burke and William Hare murdered sixteen fellow countrymen and sold their bodies to an anatomist named Robert Knox. Hare turned state's evidence and helped convict his colleague. Burke was eventually hanged and publicly dissected. To this day, his skeleton remains displayed at Edinburgh Medical

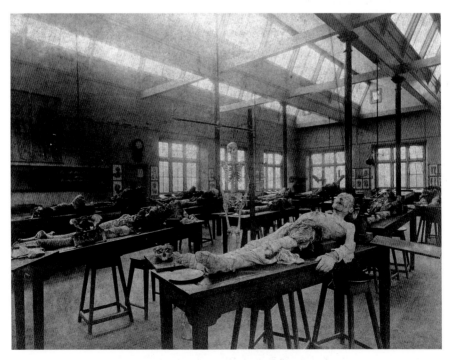

A Cambridge dissecting room (1888). *Wellcome Collection, attribution 4.0 International (CC BY 4.0).*

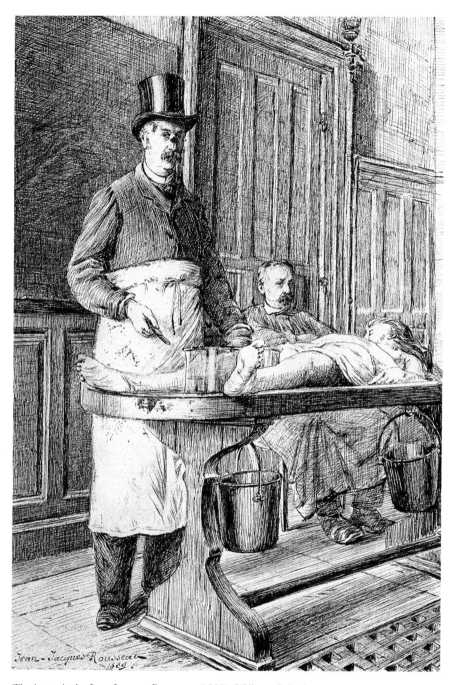

The Anatomist, by Jean-Jacques Rousseau (1889). *Wellcome Collection.*

Burke murdering one of his victims. *Wikimedia Commons.*

School. After his internationally sensational trial, the term "burking" became common in newspapers when describing graverobbing activity.

The practice was so well known in the western world, that in 1859, Charles Dickens included graverobbing in *A Tale of Two Cities*. The character named Jerry Cruncher worked full time as a porter but moonlighted as a "resurrection man."

The public outrage at graverobbing stemmed not only from religious objections but also because body snatching disrupted established customs that, according to Sappol, "ritually affirms the humanity of the dead individual."[49] Post–Civil War Gilded Age funerary practices developed to signal "respect for the personhood of the deceased. The deathbed vigil, the wake, the death shroud, burial in a coffin or tomb, embalming, served to set apart the dead person from the living, providing temporary protection from the predations of desecrators, curiosity seekers, and vermin."[50] Body snatching disrupted this.

From the end of the American Civil War through the early 1900s, Indiana newspapers reported on dozens of graverobbing cases. In December 1873, for instance, the grave of John Vollmer's daughter, who was buried at the German Catholic Cemetery in Indianapolis, was discovered as having "been rifled of its contents in the most sacrilegious manner; the casket lay broken to pieces, and the body lifted with such violence as to dislodge part of the clothing."[51] As the *Indianapolis News* concluded, "These outrages are becoming too frequent, and there seems no security against the frequent occurrence."[52]

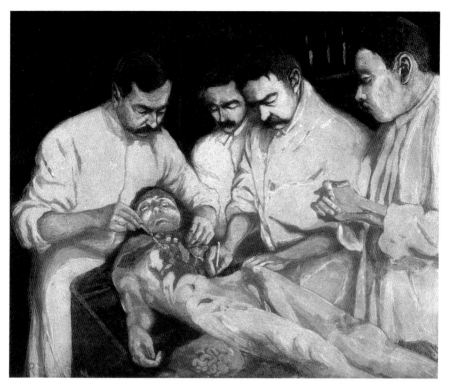

René Perrette's 1904 drawing of a dissection. *Wellcome Collection.*

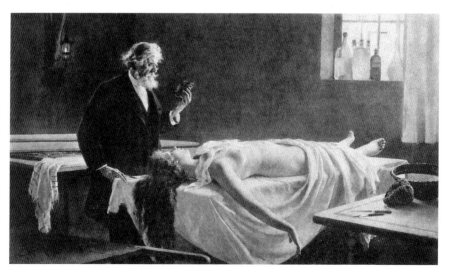

Enrique Simonet y Lombardo's lurid engraving of a 1906 dissection. *Wellcome Collection.*

One year later, in October 1874, a man "was arrested on board the east bound express train to-night for grave robbing or body snatching. His victim was the body of a young girl, whose remains were interred at Seymour yesterday."[53] In December, Indy's city sexton had "become disgusted with the grave-robbing in Greenlawn Cemetery, which he stigmatized as disgraceful, and states that he is powerless to prevent, and he recommends the appointment of two night watchmen."[54] But this never happened. In December 1875, the *News* reported that "a case of body snatching of recent occurrence at Greenlawn Cemetery, has been reported to the police authorities, in the hope of apprehending the resurrectionists."[55]

Hoosier graverobbing was so out of control in the early 1870s that the Indiana General Assembly passed laws in 1875 "defining grave robbing and prescribing punishment"[56] of such activities. However, in a pattern that was to repeat for the next thirty years, the anatomy laws did little to slow the black market trafficking of cadavers. Three years later, the *Kokomo Dispatch* reported that "grave robbing is still going on all over the country. As we before remarked, cremation is the only absolute safety."[57]

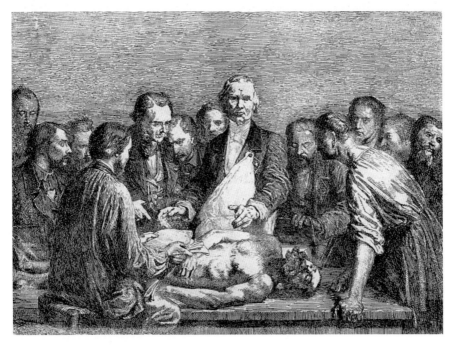

An 1864 etching of a Paris surgeon performing a dissection, by François Feyen-Perrin. *Wellcome Collection.*

Indiana Law on Grave Robbing.

The law in regard to grave-robbing is as follows:

Section 2286, Burns's Revised Statutes, 1901: Disturbing grave—Any person who shall, without due process of law, or the consent of the surviving husband or wife, or next of kin of the deceased, or of the person having control of such grave, open any grave for the purpose of taking therefrom any such dead body, or any part thereof buried therein, or anything interred therewith, shall be deemed guilty of a felony, and upon conviction thereof, shall be imprisoned in the State prison for not less than three nor more than ten years.

Section 2287, Taking Corpse.—Any person who shall, without due process of law, or the consent of the surviving husband, wife or next of kin of the deceased person, take from any grave, vault or any other burial place, any human body or any part thereof which has been interred therein, for any purpose other than for the lawful re-interment of the same, shall be deemed guilty of a felony, and, upon conviction thereof, shall be imprisoned in the State prison for not less than three or more than ten years.

Section 2288, Aiding Concealment of Corpse.—Any person who shall knowingly aid in concealing any dead body or any part thereof, which has been unlawfully taken for the purpose of dissection, shall be deemed guilty of a felony and, upon conviction thereof, shall be punished by imprisonment in the State prison for not less than one nor more than three years.

Section 2289, Buying Corpse.—Any person who shall buy or receive by gift or otherwise, any dead human body or any part thereof, knowing the same to have been disinterred and removed from its place of burial, or otherwise taken and removed in violation of this act, shall be deemed an accessory to such offense and on conviction thereof be punished in like manner as is prescribed in the preceding section of this act.

Indiana's graverobbing laws, from the *Indianapolis News*, September 29, 1902. *Hoosier State Chronicles.*

In April 1877, the body of Fred Helle was discovered missing from his grave at Prairie Grove Cemetery in Fort Wayne. The "affair has created much excitement, and the citizens are justly indignant at the outrage."[58] One year later, the body of eight-year-old William Peyton was found in a Fort Wayne medical school, stolen from a Roanoke cemetery.[59]

The General Assembly attempted to strengthen the anatomy laws again in 1879. The *Indiana State Sentinel* reported that two bills were proposed, "one relating to grave robbing and the other providing means whereby medical institutions may obtain subjects for dissection. The first makes it a felony to rob a grave, punishable with fine and imprisonment; the second, which purports to be an aid to scientific investigation, provides that medical institutions may have a dead body for the purpose of dissection if no living relatives claim the body for interment."[60] The bills became law later that year, although the *Sentinel* doubted their efficacy: "We conclude that medical colleges might hope to obtain a 'stiff' about once or twice during a century. Instead of aiding science, such legislation…would pretty effectually put a stop to all scientific investigation."[61]

The dearth of newspaper reports about graverobbing in the 1880s suggests that maybe the laws had some effect. But by the end of the decade, body snatching had returned to the Hoosier state in earnest. In February 1890, Dr. W.E. Grant and Dr. James Blackburn of the Kentucky School of Medicine were arrested for graverobbing in New Albany along with their assistant William Meaux. The school's dean suggested that "there is not necessity for the physicians to rob the graves, and that they were influenced simply by a spirit of adventure."[62] The dean's dismissal of the crime wasn't exactly shared by the people of New Albany. Nervous family members began burying loved ones "in such a manner that by means of a tube and the addition of a light it can be seen if the body has been disturbed."[63]

William Deeble, the New Albany resident who had reported the trio's graverobbing crime, began receiving threatening letters postmarked from Louisville. The first letter threatened Deeble: "[If] you give any evidence incriminating Drs. Grant and Blackburn in case of trial you will be made a fit subject for a dissecting table. Take warning."[64] The note was signed with a skull and crossbones. The letters worked. Grant and Blackburn were acquitted in April 1891.[65]

In June 1890, "Harry Insley, of Terre Haute, a young medical student, was arrested at Greencastle for alleged grave robbing."[66] Insley was studying medicine at Indiana Asbury University (now DePauw) and was the son of a "well-known Terre Haute doctor."[67] He attempted to steal the corpse of a transient man who had died recently.

Two months later, a badly decomposed body was found at a temporary embalming school in Muncie. The *Indianapolis News* reported that the body's discovery caused a sensation and "terrible rumors of murder and grave-robbing abounded for a time."[68]

North Meridian Street in 1902. The photo was taken from the monument. *From* The Journal Handbook of Indianapolis, *Indianapolis–Marion County Public Library.*

In early 1892, Otto Van Tesnar, the janitor at Central College of Physicians and Surgeons in Indy, was arrested and charged with "concealing a body that had been stolen for the purpose of dissection."[69] Tesnar had accepted the body of Emma Cossel after it was stolen from the Mount Jackson Cemetery in January. The *News* concluded the article by noting the increase in graverobbing:

> *It is now known that there has been too much of this body-snatching in this neighborhood. It used to prevail largely. To make it unnecessary, the Legislature provided means by which bodies could be had from public institutions, when no relatives put up a prior claim. Grave-robbing is now the most unnecessary of crimes in Indiana, yet there has been much of it right here in the city.*[70]

Jeff Garrigus, a well-known area ghoul, was later arrested for "robbing the grave of Emma Cossel on the night of January 18, at Mt. Jackson."[71] The judge threw out the case when prosecutors admitted that they only had circumstantial evidence. Garrigus was arrested at least twice more in Indianapolis for graverobbing, once in 1894[72] and again in 1898.[73]

In November 1892, diggers discovered widespread graverobbing at Carpenter Cemetery in Cloverland, Indiana, when they went to move the body of May West.[74] "When the workmen reached the bottom of [her] grave they found the coffin empty. It is feared that wholesale grave robbing has been going on in this cemetery for years, and the people are greatly excited."[75]

In late 1894, it was discovered that several bodies had been stolen from Greenlawn Cemetery near Franklin, Indiana, including the body of James Curry, the former Johnson County sheriff.[76] Around this same time, the state's medical colleges were lobbying members of the General Assembly for new laws that would require all public institutions—like orphanages, jails, almshouses, hospitals and asylums (ward-based mental health institutions)—to turn over *all* "bodies of persons that die at the public institutions" to the medical colleges as cadavers.[77] But the recent discoveries of body snatching "might result in defeating the bill which the colleges have intended to introduce."[78]

James Trulock, Thomas Kirk and Lee Martin were all arrested in early 1895 for the theft of Curry's body.[79] The good folks in Johnson County were having none of it. The *News* reported later in the year that "a novel way has been devised here to prevent grave robbing. Last winter, two or three graves were robbed, among them being that of the ex-sheriff. Last week the body of Mrs. W.H. Bishop was buried in Greenwood Cemetery, and in the grave with the body was placed a quantity of nitro-glycerin."[80]

Then, in September 1900, an Indiana Avenue livery stable worker by the name of John McEndree was arrested and charged with petit larceny. Indianapolis police caught McEndree late one night with graverobbing tools in his wagon. The cops didn't have enough evidence to hold him for body snatching, so they charged him with theft of the tools. When he was taken to court, he told the judge that the tools weren't his but that someone else left them in the back of the wagon. The rig, according to McEndree, had been rented by a man he did not know. When the renter failed to return, McEndree and an associate named Garfield Buckner went looking for it. They found it just outside Mount Jackson Cemetery with graverobbing tools in the back. The duo saw no one, and not wanting to discard the valuable implements, they opted to drive the rig back to the livery barn.[81] IPD patrolmen noticed the two early that morning and began following after remembering that Buckner was employed at a local medical college. At the barn, Buckner spotted the cops and ran, but McEndree stayed and wove the ridiculous claim that he had no idea where the tools came from.[82]

The case was dismissed in court the next day. Prosecutors didn't have any evidence. When the judge asked McEndree who had rented the horse rig, the ghoul gave the name Rufus Cantrell.

CHAPTER 3
BODIES GONE MISSING

A large crowd packed the courtroom on the day of the graverobbers' arraignment, Tuesday, September 30, 1902. The sensational nature of the alleged crimes and subsequent press coverage in Indianapolis newspapers brought enraged family members, curious onlookers and horrified residents to court for a glimpse of the perpetrators. Neither Rufus Cantrell nor Joseph Alexander appeared at the arraignment, but both ghouls were represented by their attorneys.

Several African Americans were among the crowd and voiced their outrage at the spectacle. The *Indianapolis Journal* reported that "each man seemed to have his own version of the law, and told in loud tones how he would treat the prisoners if he were the judge to try the cases."[83] The onlookers reserved special animosity toward Alexander, concluding that he would escape much of the blame, while the Black graverobbers would receive disproportionate penalties: "Dr. Alexander seemed to be the greatest object of their derision. They said, if it were not for the doctor, the ghouls would hardly have resorted to their wholesale robbery of graves."[84]

The grandsons of the late Johanna Stilz were also at the courthouse. Stilz had died that July. Given the recent press, her grandsons opened her grave and found it empty. Incensed family members cornered deputy prosecutor James Collins at the arraignment and demanded a search warrant, which he granted. Together with Detectives Asch and Manning, the group searched Central College for their missing grandmother, but they didn't find her body. Additional searches at other Indy-area medical

James Collins in 1912, deputy prosecutor at the time of the trials. *Library of Congress.*

colleges turned up nothing. Like Glendora Gates and so many others, Johanna Stilz's body was nowhere to be found.

That first week of October 1902 was one of citywide searches. Detectives and grieving families combed through area medical colleges, dental institutes and graveyards in search of their missing loved ones. The quests yielded little. Detectives found eight bodies during one search at Central College, but they weren't the ones they were looking for. At a second search of Central College the next day, all eight bodies had been removed. Similar occurrences happened throughout that week. The *Journal* reported on October 1:

> *At the Indiana Medical College, where it was said at least fifty bodies have been kept during the summer in anticipation of the big work of the coming season, but six bodies were found in the vats. The detectives are now firm in their belief that the college authorities have hidden the extra bodies. It has been said that the bodies may have been shipped to other towns, and yet some may be in this city. It is thought that if the cellars and stables of several doctors were searched probably some of the bodies for which search warrants have been issued would be found.*[85]

The same day as the arraignment, Cantrell led Asch and Manning on a fact-finding mission to Mount Jackson Cemetery. Together they dug into several graves, all of which were found empty, just as Cantrell said. The three were aided in their search by Mount Jackson's visibly distressed sexton, W.H. Spears, and his assistant, Adam Ault. After the graves were opened,

> *Spears and Ault at once became uneasy. When Cantrell finished his work to the satisfaction of the detectives, he turned to Spears and laughingly asked, "Oh, you need not look so scared at this work. You remember the night we tied you to the tree and then went about robbing those graves. We did not have any trouble tying you, for you got your 'dive' out of the pot."*[86]

Cantrell's implication, of course, was that sexton Spears and his assistant were in on the conspiracy. Amazingly, Cantrell even managed to get a confession out of Spears and Ault at the graveyard. Cantrell, "by his own questioning compelled Spears and Ault to admit that they had been in conversation with doctors at night in the graveyard."[87] The two also provided Asch and Manning with a description of each doctor who participated.

As evidence and testimony were collected that October, detectives developed a more complete picture of the graverobbing ring, one that revealed support, participation and complicity from many individuals at multiple levels of society. Aided by Cantrell's confessions, Asch and Manning learned that the medical college demonstrators orchestrated much of the body snatching.

On Wednesday, October 1, the prosecutor, John C. Ruckleshaus; deputy prosecutors Charles Benedict and James Collins; IPD captain Samuel Gerber; and Detectives Adolph Asch and Chauncey Manning all interviewed Cantrell and his crew. The inquiry lasted well into the afternoon. The ghouls generally corroborated everything Cantrell had disclosed during his interview. Another graverobber named Buford Cowley, who had been arrested just the day before, even admitted to stealing the body of Raphael Compitello, "the Italian murdered by negroes at Liberty and Washington streets one night last summer."[88] His body had been stolen from the German Catholic Cemetery and sold to a medical college.

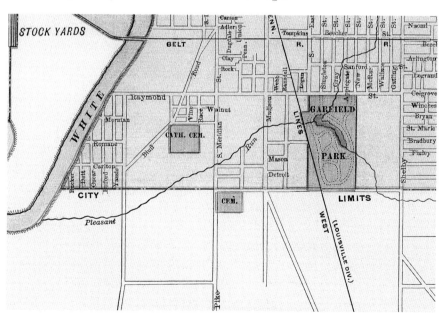

German Catholic (*left*) and Concordia Cemeteries in 1903. *Wikimedia Commons.*

The same day of the interrogation, the *Journal* discovered that Dr. Alexander had made daily visits to the Board of Health in summer, "where he scrutinized death returns closely, oftentimes taking copious notes."[89] Alexander's inquiries were "mysterious to the clerical force in the office, but Dr. Alexander being known, no questions were asked."[90] Alexander, so it seemed, was conducting market research on the recently deceased. No one considered it strange enough at the time to ask what he was doing.

As the interrogation waned into the afternoon, several Pike Township residents dug into the grave of the late Caroline Tyler of Clermont and found it empty. Tyler's nephews immediately reported the missing body to police. The nephews were issued a search warrant and, like so many others in recent weeks, scoured Central College for their missing aunt's body. The group found only one corpse at the school, that of Mary Pierce. They moved on to search the Indiana Medical College and found the same six cadavers still brining in pickling vats.[91]

It wasn't illegal for medical colleges to have bodies on hand for dissection and demonstration purposes, as long as the cadavers were obtained as the law allowed and accompanied by records of names, residences and places of origin. However, it appeared to investigators that no college was keeping the required documentation, likely on purpose to hide the trafficking. The prolific searches, even when they didn't turn up the desired corpses, made it clear to prosecutors that the city's medical colleges were disregarding the law. After the collection of sufficient evidence, prosecutor Collins charged one person at each medical college for violating the recordkeeping law: Dr. William Molt of the Physio-Medical College, Dr. John Long of the Central Dental College, Dr. Edgar Hadley of the Indiana Dental College and Dr. Frank Wright of the Eclectic Medical College of Indiana. Dr. Joseph Alexander of the Central College of Physicians and Surgeons was charged with failing to keep appropriate records. The cops also charged a few sextons and gravediggers with aiding and abetting the resurrectionists. Several other ghouls fled town when word got out about their warrants.

Around this time in early October, the *News* reported that a few families also planned civil lawsuits against the medical colleges for their culpability in masterminding the ring. Wesley Gates, the father of Glendora Gates (whose body was still missing), the family of Ebenezer Perry and the widow of Wallace Johnson all intended to sue.[92]

Cantrell gave impromptu interviews to reporters that October. I get the impression that newsmen were often allowed into jail. However, it's hard to say just how accurate these exchanges were. During one interview, as

The Indiana Dental College in 1902. *From* The Journal Handbook of Indianapolis, *Indianapolis–Marion County Public Library.*

Cantrell puffed confidently on a cigar, he supposedly told reporters, "A few years ago I became a licensed preacher of a colored Baptist mission in a small town not far from Indianapolis. Oftentimes my work brought me to this city. I can recall thirteen funerals that I attended in which I was instrumental in despoiling the same night. I'll admit that it was all hypocrisy, but I was well paid for the work; I got more money than is made out of preaching."[93]

The reporters writing this story certainly had a motivation to sensationalize an already graphic account of body snatching. Lots of people were reading the story daily in the press. Consider the audience too; the papers were widely read by Hoosiers who abhorred and feared graverobbing but also were quite familiar with it. The reporters also knew that too many readers detested Black men. Some of these "interviews" may have been written to match the reader's expectations or simply made up to sell papers. For instance, on October 3, Cantrell supposedly told reporters this grisly tale:

> *You know Minnie, that little colored girl that was struck by the street car and died; well I preached her funeral and at the same time was wondering what her relatives would think if they knew that in another day that body would be reposing in a vat at a certain medical college. I preached the sermon and was complemented by some of my efforts. That same night I went with several friends to the graveyard and "lifted" the body of the girl. There are a number of cases that I could cite where I stole the bodies while I occupied the position of a preacher.*[94]

In another story, Cantrell supposedly

> *stole the body from the house before the funeral. The undertaker, who was in on the deal, closed the coffin and all that it contained when brought to the church was a pack of playing cards. That I do think was a real cold-blooded trick. Think of my thoughts as I stood on that platform and spoke of the good deeds of the deceased, when I knew the same was resting comfortably in a pickling vat at a medical college.*[95]

Rufus later said that these two stories were false. I tend to agree. "Think of my thoughts as I stood on the platform"? Please. Did anyone actually talk like this?

There are worse accounts found in other papers, but these sinister tales were the ones published at the time in Indianapolis. Whatever the truth about the past, Cantrell was working with police detectives in locating bodies and implicating accomplices in October 1902. The ghoul was interrogated again, at length, on October 6. True to form, or at least true to the character that the newspapers had created of him, Cantrell was "laughing and seemed to be not in the least worried over the probable outcome of the serious charge against him."[96] In this session, Cantrell either confirmed or divulged that the graverobbing operations extended well beyond Indianapolis and Marion County. He disclosed that body snatching happened "throughout the gas belt, and they also say that there is a large gang of white men that have been covering this territory, robbing graves"[97] in Anderson, Alexandria, Elwood, Fairmount and Muncie. In Fairmount, Cantrell believed that white resurrectionists had stolen well over one hundred different bodies. A few days later, however, the sexton at Fairmount's Park Cemetery reported that no graves had been disturbed and certainly not one hundred of them. Perhaps Cantrell was confused as to which cemetery—maybe he lied or exaggerated, or possibly he just got the wrong place. Maybe the sexton lied.

Cantrell led Asch and Manning on yet another quest for evidence on October 8. That afternoon, they searched, once again, at the Central Medical College of Physicians and Surgeons. Cantrell found several human bones charred in the furnace, leading the detectives to believe that "the college authorities have burned the bodies that were in their possession ten days ago."[98] They followed by searching funeral homes but found nothing.

Cantrell's searches with the detectives became a bit of a cause célèbre. One trip to search an area mortuary generated a great deal of attention, as "the sight of Rufus Cantrell walking up Indiana avenue in company with the detectives was appreciated by many colored men and boys, who formed a procession and followed the searching party."[99]

Rufus also provided detectives with more details about bodies lifted from Mount Jackson and the German Catholic cemeteries. Once again, Detectives Asch and Manning traveled to the graveyards with Rufus to ascertain the validity of his claims. The *Journal* reported that "while in the Mount Jackson graveyard Cantrell said that the bodies of Dorie Snowden, Albert Tanner, Ed Johnson and several other men, had been taken to the medical colleges instead of being buried. [Cantrell] said the coffins were buried with large pieces of ice in them to make them heavy."[100] After opening Snowden's grave, the detectives found it empty.

From there, the trio moved to German Catholic Cemetery, where Cantrell led detectives to the grave of Katherine Derringer, buried not six weeks prior. Her grave was found empty after it was opened. Cantrell pointed to white resurrectionists as the culprits.

Cemeteries across central Indiana began internal investigations that yielded little. John Chislett, the superintendent of Crown Hill Cemetery, emphatically denounced rumors that graverobbing had taken place in the city's preeminent cemetery. Chislett told reporters:

> Such "pipedreams" as that printed this afternoon are vicious and should not be permitted to reach the eyes of the public. That whole story is untrue and I think it is like others of the same character printed in the same paper…the cemetery is too well policed for any ghoul to attempt to steal a body from a grave. Not since my connection with the association have I learned of anyone trying to get into the cemetery at night. Any one found prowling about the place would be instantly shot if a satisfactory explanation was not offered.[101]

Circa 1900 photo of the Crown Hill Cemetery entrance. *Library of Congress.*

For twenty years, Crown Hill had employed night watchmen, installing them as a "precaution against such a thing occurring in that cemetery a number of years ago."[102] The cemetery also installed a call box system, where the watchmen recorded their position in the cemetery as they made patrols. The boxes were installed so that each guard had to report every ten minutes as he made the rounds. They carried revolvers and were instructed to "shoot to kill if the prowler should fail to give an account of why he is there."[103]

At Muncie's Beach Grove Cemetery, superintendent O.W. Crabbs responded to rumors about an internal cemetery investigation. Published in the *Muncie Morning Star,* Crabbs wrote:

> *I am positive that Beech Grove cemetery has not been visited by ghouls. There has been a watchman in the cemetery each night and at no time has there been any evidence of molestation of the graves. The report sent out from Muncie to an Indianapolis paper, saying that Beech Grove cemetery would be investigated, is absolutely false. We will make no investigation, for it is unnecessary.*[104]

Above: Hibben, Hollweg & Company, where two dead bodies were found tied in sacks. *From* The Journal Handbook of Indianapolis, *Indianapolis–Marion County Public Library.*

Opposite: Rand McNally map of Indy from 1903. *Wikimedia Commons.*

Given the prolific number of empty graves in Indianapolis, detectives and family members knew that the bodies of their loved ones had been stolen, even if their corpses hadn't turned up yet at a medical college. Detectives concluded that along with burning several bodies, the colleges also might have quickly sold them to other communities in the area—shuttled out via the electric interurbans or on steam powered inter-city railroads.

Such suspicions led detectives to search farther afield. On October 8, thirty dead bodies were found hanging from meat hooks in a Louisville ice cream factory. The corpses were held in a cold storage building out back, as the "same pipes which were used in congealing the cream for table use were connected up with a small plant in a shed in the rear where they kept the bodies cool."[105] Louisville-area medical colleges had contracted with Wathen's Ice Cream to keep the bodies chilled. Detectives Asch and Manning negotiated permission to search the building, despite assurances from both local police and medical colleges that all bodies had been obtained legally. They determined that none of the corpses at the ice cream plant was a cadaver missing from Indianapolis.

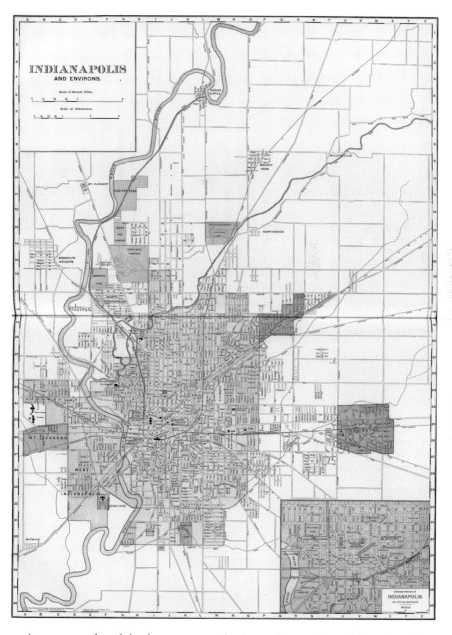

A gruesome break in the case came in the early morning of October 14 as Amos Smith walked to work downtown. Rounding the corner at Meridian and Georgia Streets, Smith discovered two corpses tied up in sacks outside Hibben, Hollweg and Company's dry goods store. Smith, naturally alarmed at finding sacks of corpses at 5:30 a.m., ran a little farther south for help and stumbled across two other bags of dead bodies at the back entrance of Central College. A frantic Smith phoned the police, who sent a bicycle patrolman to investigate. The bodies were sent to the city morgue and identified as Catherine (Catarina) Doehring, Wallace Johnson, Johanna Stilz and Glendora Gates.

Gates was missing jewelry and gold teeth. The other families were able to identify the remains of their loved ones, except for Wallace Johnson's family. If you can believe it, the police brought in Rufus Cantrell to confirm the body's identity, which he promptly did.[106]

The day before the horrifying discovery, the police denied allegations that the investigation was being called off. A rumor circulated that "certain doctors connected with the medical colleges…asked that further investigation be discontinued."[107] Alas, the grand jury investigation had begun the same day and with it, the fate of Rufus Cantrell and his accomplices.

CHAPTER 4

THE GRAND JURY

T he grand jury empaneled in mid-October 1902 weighed all evidence to assess the criminality of the ghouls and their medical school colleagues. On the morning of October 13, criminal court judge Freemont Alford instructed grand jurors to "first take up the investigation of all persons charged with the crime of disturbing the graves, stealing corpses and of all persons aiding in the concealment of corpses so stolen in Marion County."[108]

Charles Benedict, the deputy prosecutor, led the questioning of witnesses. The grand jury itself consisted of members from across Marion County, including Peter Bank from Wayne Township; William Schliecher from Warren Township; John Schley, James Chapin and Charles Kahl from Center Township; and Talbott Moore from Pike Township.[109] After a week, it was discovered that Moore was the cousin of W.H. Spears, the Mount Jackson Cemetery sexton whom Cantrell accused of aiding the ghouls. The *Journal* noted that Moore would not let familial bonds cloud his judgment—"that this fact of relationship would not interfere with his just and conscientious consideration of the investigation, and if the evidence submitted to the grand jury justified it he would not hesitate to return indictments against the guilty persons."[110]

Detectives Asch and Manning were the first to give testimony on October 13. Cantrell was to follow. In a typical mix of racism and sensationalism, the *Indianapolis News* reported:

Right: Charles Benedict in 1897, deputy prosecutor during the trials. *Library of Congress.*

Below: The Marion County Courthouse, where most of the ghouls' trials were held. *From* The Journal Handbook of Indianapolis, *Indianapolis–Marion County Public Library.*

MARION COUNTY COURT HOUSE.

Cantrell reached the court house at 9 o'clock in the charge of Deputy Sheriff Comer. He asked to be allowed to visit the office of the assessor of Center township, as he had a friend there who he desired to have a short chat. The big negro walked into the assessor's office with an air of independent bravado and stuck out his hand to shake hands with one of the deputies. He met a cold repulse by a former friend.[111]

Cantrell then met with the grand jury, answering questions from deputy prosecutor Benedict. The ghoul was accompanied by his lawyer, Cass Connaway. As the papers reported it, Cantrell was forthcoming, direct and jovial during the proceedings. His "enthusiasm in making his disclosures to the six investigators was evident by the loud tone of voice in which he frequently talked. He could be heard in the corridor of the court house, but his words were not understood. Cantrell was apparently in high spirits, for his story to the grand jury was frequently interrupted by laughter. Cantrell acts as though he is having a holiday."[112]

It's hard to make sense of his joviality. He later claimed that he was drunk during the testimony, but plenty of eyewitnesses said that he was stone sober. I tend to think that Rufus Cantrell was just a charismatic guy, charming many who knew him. I get the impression from the newspaper reports that he was well liked on a personal level by everyone, including the cops. To the grand jury, he divulged what he knew, laying "particular stress on the point that he was employed to do the work and was well paid for it by the physicians that employed him."[113]

Cantrell revealed to those empaneled what information he had disclosed to Asch and Manning, plus additional details about white graverobbers who were active across central Indiana. He supposedly had evidence of one such gang, but when he returned to his "home to collect it, it was gone."[114]

The papers hinted that the city's medical establishment continued in its efforts to derail the investigation. A rumor began circulating that Dr. Eugene Buehler, the secretary of Indy's Board of Health, threatened prosecutor John Ruckelshaus that if he "was overly zealous in performing his duties as prosecutor and securing the indictment of Dr. Joseph Alexander for being an accessory to the ghouls…the physicians of the Central College would try to defeat his re-election."[115]

Buehler denied the charge, telling the *Journal* that "I never threatened Ruckelshaus." He added, "The faculty of the Central College of Physicians and Surgeons told him that the members of the faculty would provide the necessary money to employ counsel for Alexander and would use every

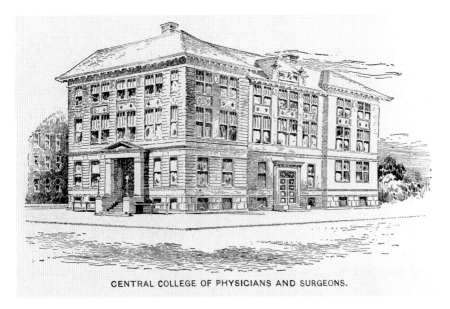

CENTRAL COLLEGE OF PHYSICIANS AND SURGEONS.

A 1902 etching of the Central College of Physicians and Surgeons. *From* The Journal Handbook of Indianapolis, *Indianapolis–Marion County Public Library.*

honorable means to secure his release from the charge."[116] Buehler then deployed some old-fashioned American racism to defend his colleague:

> *At the faculty meeting at which it was decided to support Alexander, twenty-five of the leading physicians of the city, members of the college faculty and other physicians not connected with the school, were present, and it was the unanimous opinion that the word of Dr. Alexander, whom we recognize as a friend and professional brother, should be supported instead of the word of a negro who was discharged from the United States Army for insanity, and who has certainly lied in many particulars since the investigation started.*[117]

Mid-month, a clerk of the Board of County Commissioners told police that he had stumbled on some ghouls the previous November on his way home from work. "The night was dark and cold. Suddenly he encountered four men, walking across the road. They carried something between them and when Norwood approached, they dropped it. It was a corpse."[118] One of the ghouls told the clerk, "You skate and skate quick."[119] Although Norwood reported the incident, the body was never recovered.

The grand jury questioned several other witnesses and accused co-conspirators, but not everyone. Dr. Alexander didn't sit for an interview, as he was "advised by his attorney to not enter the investigation until he is required to defend himself under an indictment."[120] Sam Martin, on advice from his attorney, also refused to answer questions but later acquiesced.

Cantrell was called back to testify on October 20. The ghoul revealed to the grand jury that he had once worked at a Louisville medical college, officially to prepare cadavers for dissection but, in reality, to steal them from graves. Rufus had even gone to Louisville with a letter of introduction "from certain Indianapolis physicians to Dr. Edward L. David, registrar of the Louisville medical college."[121] Cantrell's body snatching operations didn't work out in Louisville "because he had white men under him."[122]

Cantrell told the grand jurors, "I went to work preparing subjects for dissection in the medical department of the University of Louisville, at Eighth and Chestnut streets, and at the Kentucky School of Medicine on Walnut Street. I was in close touch with the gangs, however. About a month later I got ready to come home, and Dr. David gave me a letter [to give to the Louisville mayor], who furnished me with a ticket."[123] Incredibly, the mayor of Louisville gave the body snatcher a train ticket home!

Dr. David did, in fact, remember Cantrell but emphatically denied that the school was involved in graverobbing to obtain cadavers. David told the *Journal* that "body snatching was not necessary in Kentucky, as the State furnished all bodies legitimately."[124]

As October rolled along, Indianapolitans besieged Asch and Manning with requests to open tombs across the city. The detectives didn't have the personnel to disinter every grave, so they told callers that "the only way to ascertain the truth is to open the graves" themselves.[125] The detectives also began receiving anonymous tips, including a letter "saying that the body of the wife of the Rev. C.A. Penick, pastor of the African-Methodist church in Norwood, was stolen from Lick Creek cemetery several months ago."[126]

Then on October 20, IPD patrolmen discovered "human remains in several barrels of garbage that an old negro deposited last Saturday at the 'dumps' in the northwestern part of the city." Police found feet, arms and "the trunk of a man" in the barrels. The body parts were partially burned, perhaps as an attempt to conceal them. "They theory that someone connected with the recent grave robberies has taken this method of disposing of bodies."[127]

About this same time, a report from a special commission was filed in Judge George Stubbs's police court. Commissioners were tasked with

The Medical College of Indiana in 1902. *From* The Journal Handbook of Indianapolis, *Indianapolis–Marion County Public Library.*

determining why ten corpses were buried in the basement of the Medical College of Indiana. The bodies had been unearthed during one of Asch and Manning's earlier searches. The commissioners found that the corpses weren't part of the ring but had been partially destroyed in a fire four years prior and buried. The doctors at the college wanted to "have the cadavers cleaned and the bones preserved for the use of students who might wish to retain them for their personal use." However, a janitor tasked with the cleaning "became intoxicated and buried the ten bodies."[128] Mystery solved.

On Saturday, October 25, the Marion County grand jury submitted its findings to Judge Alford. It returned twenty-five indictments, including several against Cantrell, most of his ghouls, other co-conspirators and five Indianapolis physicians. The grand jurors accused the graverobbers with:

Unlawfully and feloniously removing and taking from the grave of a deceased person, the dead body of such deceased person, for a purpose

other than lawful internment of the same, to wit: for the purpose of
barter and sale to the Central College of Physicians and Surgeons, there
being such, so removed as aforesaid, without due process of law and
without the consent of the surviving husband or wife, or next of kin of
such deceased person.[129]

Within three days, the accused who were not already in custody were arrested and formally indicted. Many of the resurrectionists appeared in court locked in handcuffs to plead not guilty. Cantrell indicated that he wasn't prepared to enter a plea, but the clerk went ahead and recorded not guilty.[130] The five doctors, however, were not to be "arraigned until the day of their trial."[131]

Dr. Frank Wright, secretary and treasurer of the Eclectic Medical College, was indicted for accepting two corpses on behalf of the college on October 10, 1901: a man with the surname Moore and the body of John Sargent. Wright was accused of paying Cantrell twenty-five dollars each for the corpses. Dr. Joseph Alexander was indicted for accepting the bodies of Glendora Gates on July 10, 1902; Rose Neidlinger on August 21, 1902; and Stella Middletown on August 25.[132]

Herman Fritz, a bartender at the North Street Saloon, was accused of concealing a body at the saloon until it could be delivered to Eclectic Medical College. William McElroy, Bud Richardson and James Harvey were also indicted for helping the bartender conceal the body. An undertaker by the

Freemont Alford in 1912, Indianapolis judge. *Library of Congress.*

name of Cassius Willis, who ran a mortuary on Indiana Avenue; his assistant James Harvey; and the janitor at Central College, William Haymaker, were all indicted for trafficking dead bodies. The Mount Jackson Cemetery sexton, W.H. Spears, was accused of two counts of concealing a dead body. His gravedigger and night watchman, Adam Ault, was indicted with stealing the body of Adline Best.[133]

The jury indicted Dr. John Wilson, internist at Central College, with three counts of concealing a body, that of Glendora Gates on July 10, 1902; Catherine Doehring on August 20, 1902; and Joanna Stilz on August 27, 1902. Dr. William Molt, demonstrator

Early twentieth-century Indy Police Department wagon. *Indianapolis–Marion County Public Library.*

at the Physio Medical College, was indicted on three counts each for concealing, accepting and purchasing the bodies of George Weaver and Edward Pedigo on January 10, 1902. A few days later, Dr. Charles Byrkit of Castleton was arrested for aiding Dr. Molt and indicted for the same crimes. Keep in mind that Molt, Wright and Alexander still faced charges of not keeping appropriate cadaver records as required by law.[134]

Cantrell, Buford Cowley, Walter Daniels, Sol Grady, William Jones, Samuel Martin and Isom Donnell were already being held. Additional charges were added in lieu of the grand jury's report. Bail for the seven incarcerated African Americans had been set at $1,000 each—an enormous sum in those days for most and one that Cantrell and the other body snatchers could not afford. The court set the doctors' bails high as well, $1,000 for Molt and Wright, $400 for Wilson and $1,500 for Alexander. All four doctors posted bail themselves or had support from friends and colleagues through bondsmen.[135]

The state dropped the charges against Garfield Buckner and Cornelius Jones, Mount Jackson Cemetery's gravedigger. Late in the month, the cops made a few additional arrests when new evidence became available. With a tip from Cantrell, Walter Harding was arrested and charged with stealing the body of Edward Pedigo from the Bridgeport Cemetery and another person with the surname Cress from Round Hill Cemetery. Harding confessed during questioning.

The court set Dr. Alexander's trial for November 17.

CHAPTER 5

NOVEMBER 1902

T he month of November began with the arrest of another well-known graverobber, John McEndree. You'll remember McEndree from the end of chapter 2 when, in 1900, he was arrested and acquitted for possession of "stolen" graverobbing tools. In the fall of 1902, Manning and Asch apprehended the ghoul on another tip from Cantrell. For weeks, Rufus had claimed that white ghouls had been operating in Greater Indianapolis with impunity but couldn't offer detectives sufficient evidence for arrests. Yet, whatever he told Asch and Manning in late October was enough for the detectives to bring McEndree in for questioning.[136]

The detectives arrested McEndree in Martinsville, where he had gone to hide after learning about his warrant. He first claimed total ignorance of graverobbing, but after some intense questioning, the ghoul admitted to snatching at least twenty bodies in 1901 from Cherry Grove Cemetery, Anderson Cemetery and Jones Chapel Cemetery. The ghoul admitted to recently stealing and selling the bodies of Fred Honeycut, Julia Rogers, Red Kelly, Adelina Best, Willis Long, Frank Press, Ebenezer Perry, Caroline Tyler, Perry Shaw, Hopewell Shaw, John Sargent and Peter Hutson. He couldn't remember the names of the rest. McEndree sold Ebenezer Perry's body to Central College, where it was "placed in a barrel."[137] Just before Perry's relatives searched the school, McEndree "took the body away from the college to the rear of the drug store on the North Side, where it remained for several days."[138] *Several days?* How did no one notice?

Early twentieth-century IPD wagon. *Library of Congress.*

Later in the day, Asch and Manning arrested Albert Hunt, another graverobber who ran with Cantrell. Hunt claimed that he went on only one trip and was tasked with watching horses. However, if the papers are to be believed, Hunt knew McEndree well. At least, that's what readers were to glean from a supposed jailhouse discussion as reported in the *Journal*, although the conversation seems very on the nose:

> *When McEndree was placed behind the bars he met Hunt and the two laughed heartily over their incarceration. The two men looked at one another and said: "This is all Rufus' work." Cantrell was outside the door, laughing heartily. When he heard the men talking he also took part in the conversation and said: "Boys, I did the snitching. We might as well all give in, they've got us right." McEndree and Hunt seemed to agree with Cantrell and took their arrest good-naturedly.*[139]

The detectives were "of the opinion that several more important arrests of white men will soon be made"[140] and estimated that only "one-third of the men interested in robbing graves have been arrested."[141] The remaining suspects, Asch and Manning believed, were mostly white but probably "left this part of the country since Cantrell's exposé."[142]

One day later, the *Journal* reported that the detectives arrested a druggist and medical student named Charles Riggs, this time on a tip from McEndree. Riggs admitted that he had gone with Cantrell, McEndree and several others to steal the body of John Sargent, but that it only "was for a lark."[143] Riggs, who was twenty-two years old at the time of his arrest, was definitely not the mastermind behind the operation, but his involvement reveals something significant about body snatching: it was common and considered adventurous for young men studying in the medical profession to take part in robbing graves. The culture at medical colleges supported, maintained and encouraged graverobbing.

Riggs, a onetime student at Central College, said that "the subject of grave-robbing was discussed by the students of the college frequently, and oftentimes students would accompany Cantrell and his party to escape the bantering of the older students. It was one of the freshmen or juniors who were asked to go with the grave robbers."[144] Riggs also disclosed that during the resurrection of Sargent's body, the ghouls were "accompanied by Dr. Kincaid, a former student at the Central Medical College."[145]

Astonishingly, Dr. Clarence Kincaid turned himself in the next day, telling police "that he understood he was wanted for graverobbing."[146] Kincaid admitted to tagging along on one ghoulish excursion "more in the spirit of bravado than anything else."[147] Kincaid claimed that he waited on the outskirts of the cemetery as the ghouls did their work. He was charged and released after paying the $500 bail.

Later in the week, Cantrell led Asch and Manning on another cemetery fact-finding mission. The trio went to Fall Creek Cemetery and met with a "Sexton Whistler" about empty graves. Whistler oddly, or perhaps conveniently, did not have records of *any* burials. Cantrell, "while standing with the party, pointed to several graves and said that they were empty. One of the graves was opened and found to contain an empty box."[148]

Cantrell then led detectives to North Ebenezer Cemetery, where they found the new graves of Johanna Stilz, Wallace Johnson and John Sargent undisturbed after their recent reburials.[149] At the Herron Cemetery, the sexton told Asch and Manning that ghouls had "robbed bodies from forty graves." Cantrell stood nearby and "a smile spread over his face."[150] After surveying empty graves at Round Hill and Lick Creek Cemeteries, Rufus told the detectives that he was "of opinion that more than 150 have been stolen from these two cemeteries."[151]

By the end of the day, Asch and Manning had enough evidence to make arrests of "six or seven white men"[152] who were guilty of robbing graves on behalf of Dr. Joseph Alexander, but it's not clear if the IPD made these arrests. The next week, however, the detectives did apprehend William Moffett, whom Rufus labeled as "the king of the grave robbers."[153] Moffett was a known ghoul in Indianapolis, and according to Cantrell, the veteran body snatcher had taught Rufus the tricks of the trade. As a cover, Moffett had been a "custodian of one of the medical colleges."[154]

William Moffett was remembered well by older police officers, as he was a central witness in the murder trial of William Merrick. In the fall of 1878, Merrick had killed his wife, Julia, and their newborn child. Their badly decomposed bodies were discovered several weeks after the murders. The day before Julia went missing, Merrick had purchased "ten cents worth of strychnine at the drug store."[155] A saloonkeeper on Indiana Avenue witnessed Merrick stopping for "a glass of whisky for himself and a glass of blackberry wine, the latter he said for his wife."[156] The bartender saw "Merrick empty a powder into the glass and hand it to the woman in the vehicle."[157] Merrick was later hanged for his crime.

Merrick was also a prolific body snatcher, having engaged in the practice since the 1870s, supposedly to supplement his livery stable income. The *Indianapolis News* reported in 1879 that Merrick "took to this naturally as a duck does to water, and in a short time he became the acknowledged head and font of the body snatchers in the city."[158]

As a witness in Merrick's trial, William Moffett was remembered by IPD veterans who worked the case back in the 1870s. The cops reminisced to reporters that right before Merrick's execution, he:

> *told of the grave robbing expeditions in which Moffett had figured at that time—more than twenty years ago. Merrick said that Moffett had oftentimes taken a horse and carriage and with spades and sacks had driven to the cemeteries at night and robbed graves. He was assisted in this work by Jeff Garrigus, who has the reputation of being a white ghoul.*[159]

The detectives also arrested Leroy Williams on another tip from Cantrell. Williams was apprehended at Hendrick's Café on West Washington Street, where he worked as a cook. Williams admitted to police that he took four trips with Cantrell, including the expeditions to steal the bodies of Wallace Johnson from Ebenezer Cemetery and Meredith McMullen from Lick Creek Cemetery.[160]

On November 11, Asch and Manning took Cantrell and Sam Martin to confirm this information. After opening the graves of Hubbard McMullen,

Above: Indianapolis City Building in 1902. *From* The Journal Handbook of Indianapolis, *Indianapolis–Marion County Public Library.*

Left: Sam Martin's mugshot photo from 1903. *Indiana State Archives.*

Edward Jones and Penney Whitefield at the Lick Creek Cemetery, the graves were "found to contain nothing but pine boxes."[161] The detectives led the ghouls to a few other cemeteries, where they found the same. At Round Hill Cemetery, the graves of Redmon Kelly and a mother and daughter were all found empty.[162]

Cantrell admitted to stealing these bodies with McEndree, remembering "the case very well, as a double funeral was held. He said he attended the funeral, driving out to the graveyard a little in the rear of the regular procession. He said he had marked the graves and on the second night he returned with his accomplices to steal the two bodies."[163]

A few days later, Asch and Manning arrested a rural Hamilton County farmer by the name of Hampton West. Cantrell had outed West to detectives as one of the white ghouls operating in the Greater Indianapolis area. West was lured to Indy by Asch and Manning, who asked the Hamilton County ghoul to testify in front of a grand jury. He was arrested when he showed up. The court set his bail at $2,500.[164]

West had a storied biography. He was born around 1840 to a family of squatters in North Carolina. After the onset of the American Civil War, he volunteered for the Confederate army and served under General Thomas "Stonewall" Jackson. During the Battle of Chancellorsville, West's unit accidentally fired on its commander, wounding him. Jackson died of pneumonia one week later from a botched amputation. West himself was shot in his cheek during the ensuing chaos, "disfiguring him in a manner that made him very repulsive in his appearance."[165]

Hampton and his brother William both deserted the Confederate army after this and moved to Franklin, Indiana. West didn't make any friends there, perhaps because he was a former Confederate living in a Union state in the middle of the War of the Rebellion. The *Journal* wrote that the ghoul "became such a notorious character that in a short time the residents of that place warned him and his brother to leave."[166]

The Wests took heed and resettled in Castleton, just north of Indianapolis. Hampton moved again in 1880, this time to Mudsock—the informal nickname given to Fisher's Station in Hamilton County. Fisher's Station was later shortened, as you probably know, to just Fishers in 1908. West's notorious character didn't earn him any friends in Hamilton County either, although he opened a saloon in 1880 and earned the nickname "Hamp."[167]

Like Merrick, Moffett and Garrigus, West was remembered by IPD veterans as a longtime Indianapolis graverobber. Older detectives also recalled that West killed "the best damn man in Mudsock."[168] The *Journal* wrote in 1902:

> *One day in the early spring a notorious character named Ab Lynn walked into the saloon and declared that he was "the best damn man in Mudsock." He offered to whip every man in the saloon to corroborate his statement. West, who was behind the bar, took up the challenge. Walking from behind the counter, West picked up a bung starter[169] and assaulted Lynn, striking him on the head and crushing his skull. Lynn died shortly afterward. West was arrested for the crime, but was acquitted.[170]*

West did, in fact, kill "the best damn man in Mudsock," although the story is more complex than what the *Journal* recalled. On Saturday, February 19, 1881, a day-long brawl took place in Fisher's Station that caused the death of a man named Benjamin Fouch. "The fuss was started before noon on Saturday last, over a trivial affair, by Barney Reiner and an unknown man bearing the nick-name 'Dutch Joe.'"[171] The historical record does not say what the "trivial affair" was, but brawling between groups loyal to Dutch Joe and Reiner carried on into the afternoon. Alcohol was a major factor.

Later in the day, fighting broke out again at Andy Farrell's Saloon. This time, Hamp West and Bob Dawson were involved in the melee. West was badly beaten and, with Dawson, retreated to recover at the Confederate's saloon near the railroad. Later that evening, West's adversaries, including Benjamin Fouch and Daniel Lynn, made their way to his bar. West locked the door preventing their entry, but Dawson let them in anyway. "Fouch then walked up to the bar behind where West was standing, and with knucks still on, he brought his hand down upon the counter and said, 'I am the best damned man in Mudsock, and can whip any son of a bitch in it.'"[172] Cowering, West "insisted he did not want any further trouble, and when Fouch requested him to set up the drinks he did so without ceremony."[173]

Demonstrating that toxic masculinity was as prevalent in the late nineteenth century as it is today, Dawson then approached Daniel Lynn with a knife in his hand and said, "My dear boy, I knew your mother, and am going to kiss you for her." Dawson then tried to stab Lynn, reigniting the epic Mudsock brawl, this time involving thirty bar patrons. The *Noblesville Ledger* wrote that "billiard balls and missiles of various descriptions flew so rapidly and recklessly that all present had business elsewhere."[174]

In the middle of this ruckus, Dawson grabbed and held down Fouch. West then hit him hard in the head with a "copper beer faucet,"[175] causing

Fouch to become as "limber as a rag."[176] Dawson then grabbed Adam Lynn, and West hit him in the head too. Lynn survived, but Fouch died early the next day. The ghoul later claimed that he was acting in self-defense and that Fouch had tried to kill him. A grand jury later issued eighteen indictments against the participants, but not against Hamp West, as the jurors agreed that his act of killing "was in self defense."[177]

Between the killing and his graverobbing arrest in 1902, West occasionally appeared in local newspapers, mostly for criminal matters. For instance, in 1891, he was acquitted in *State v. Hampton West* on provocation charges.[178] West was arrested in 1895 for an "alleged assault with intent to kill Samuel Price,"[179] who was having an affair with Hamp's wife. When the ghoul learned about it, West "pounded his man into insensibility."[180]

Then in 1897, a man by the name of Thomas Roby told West that he had access to U.S. Treasury printing plates to counterfeit paper money. Roby offered the ghoul some of the "perfect notes" for a fee, to which West agreed to pay. The two met up in Indianapolis, where Hamp handed over fifty dollars to Roby, who promptly disappeared. West waited two hours and then, in either fantastic stupidity or perhaps stubborn arrogance, reported the "theft" to police.[181]

At some point in the late nineteenth century, West became a prolific graverobber, working closely with William Moffett. He became a competitor to Cantrell in 1901. During one graverobbing excursion in southern Hamilton County, Rufus and Sam Martin were "pounced upon by West and Moffett."[182] A small gun battle ensued over the corpse: "[T]he men separated and after the negroes had started toward the road the white ghouls fired on them. The negroes returned fire and for fifteen minutes, a pitched battle was carried on in the cemetery."[183] West and Moffett made off with the body.

West admitted to the detectives that "every farmer in Hamilton county looked on him as a ghoul, but none had the courage to openly accuse him of such deeds."[184] Cantrell agreed, telling reporters that "West had attended every funeral in the vicinity of his home. He had the reputation among the Hamilton county farmers of being a ghoul."[185]

Earlier in the week, William Moffett became a free man when he was inadvertently released after paying the $1,000 bail. Upon discovering the error, Asch and Manning rearrested the ghoul, and this time bail was set at $5,000. Perhaps sensing the inevitable predicament he was in, "Moffett acknowledged that he had been in the grave robbing business for thirty years and had made considerable money out of it."[186]

Moffett also admitted to working with Cantrell to steal the bodies of Martha McLaughlin and Meredith McMullen from Lick Creek Cemetery in July 1902. Upon hearing this, Asch and Manning opened the graves to confirm, and sure enough, the detectives found two empty coffins. Cantrell "said the bodies had been taken to the Central Medical College."[187]

In mid-November, Rufus stopped assisting Asch and Manning, and for good reason. Far more leniency was given to white ghouls than to Cantrell and his accomplices of color, even though they had fully cooperated with the investigation. Cantrell told reporters that it was:

> no use trying to use him for a tool any longer, as he had been duped enough. He said he had been told that the detectives would not give him the promised leniency and that he with the remainder of the negro ghouls, would suffer in prison while the white ghouls, whom he declares are more guilty than he, will be allowed to go free.[188]

Cantrell also hinted to reporters of a much larger conspiracy. He said that "the white men, if allowed to talk, would incriminate more well-known doctors in the stealing of bodies than the profession would like to have. It is for this reason, he said, that money was quickly put up with the Surety Company for the release of [West and Moffett]," both of whom had been released under bond.[189]

On November 17, Cantrell was hauled in front of a grand jury again. As he was being led into chambers, Cantrell told a reporter that he was getting "tired of this talking before the grand jury."[190] This was only partially true, as Rufus had no problem telling another outlandish story to jurors:

> One of the stories told by Cantrell today was that his gang was at the new Bethel cemetery one night. Martin, one of the colored ghouls, had a new spade. The ground was very hard, and Martin worked with such strength that he broke the spade. Nothing daunted, Martin made his way to the home of the sexton of the graveyard and asked for a spade. He explained that a crowd of "possum" hunters had run a "possum" into a hole in the ground and that they wanted a spade to dig him out. The sexton believed the story and gave Martin the spade.[191]

A day after Cantrell's testimony, the mayor of Indianapolis, Charles Bookwalter, paid Rufus a visit in jail. It's possible that Mayor Bookwalter knew Cantrell. At the very least, Cantrell was a onetime supporter of the

Republican mayor. Rufus in 1900 was the president of the Bookwalter Colored Club, a political society of Black residents who supported Bookwalter's bid for mayor.[192]

The mayor's office had received a letter from the mother of the late Walter Weddel, a young boy who had died recently and was buried at Mount Jackson Cemetery. Weddel's mother, who now lived in St. Louis, had been following the case in the papers and asked the mayor's office to assess whether the ghouls had taken her son. Cantrell remembered the death and told the mayor "that the body was too small for the ghouls to handle."[193] In such cases, Cantrell told Bookwalter, a lump of coal was placed on the tombstone to let other body snatchers know that the corpse, for whatever reason, wasn't worth taking or had already been stolen.[194]

Charles Bookwalter, mayor of Indy from 1901 to 1903 and 1906 to 1910. *Indianapolis–Marion County Public Library.*

Around this time, an unnamed lawyer also visited Cantrell in jail. The attorney "agreed to furnish [Cantrell] bond if he would leave the city."[195] Cantrell rejected the offer and would not accept support "unless it was also furnished for the other negro ghouls."[196] It's possible that Cantrell made this story up, or maybe his lawyer Cass Connaway did. To my mind, though, it seems more likely that Cantrell's disclosures and the recent arrests of the white ghouls made several prominent doctors nervous. It's quite conceivable that he was offered a bribe to skip town. Rufus, however, held his ground.[197]

Prosecutors charged Charles Riggs, Walter Williams, Hampton West, William Moffett and Clarence Kincaid with graverobbing. Garfield Buckner was recharged and arrested again under new evidence. The *News* reported that "there is enough evidence to return indictments against all the men, although it is probable that Riggs and Kincaid will not be indicted."[198]

Early in the month, a veterinarian from Hamilton County named William T. Long was deputized by the Indianapolis police to assist in the investigation.[199] Long, the brother-in-law of Wallace Johnson, whose body was found in a sack some weeks prior, was raising money to help the living victims sue the medical colleges. Long asked for donations from several Hamilton County residents, Hamp West's home turf. The *Journal* reported that West "has borne the reputation among the Hamilton county farmers

Martin Hugg in 1912, one of Alexander's lawyers. *Library of Congress.*

of being a grave robber, and it is thought on account of the high feeling against him, much money will be raised."[200]

In this same article, the *Journal* told the story of an unnamed farmer, "living three miles south of Three Notch Road," who stumbled on graverobbers at Round Hill Cemetery in 1902. The farmer told detectives that they were "looking for the bodies of Mrs. Bremmer and her daughter."[201] The countryman went to inform the sexton, but "a colored man holding a pistol at his head caused him to change his mind."[202] The men absconded with both corpses.

As for Dr. Alexander, his trial was pushed to December after his lawyers successfully argued for a change of venue. Judge Alford appointed J.M. Bailey as special judge.[203] Alexander's team of lawyers was paid for by the faculty at Central College and included William and Pertle Herod, Joseph Kealing and Martin Hugg.[204]

Alexander also caught the ire of Hamilton County farmers in late November. Several attended the pretrial hearings and "expressed their indignation at the operations of the ghouls and their sympathy for the families which have been robbed of their dead, and discussed the probable outcome of the trial of Alexander."[205]

Detectives also arrested George Mason, a well digger who had been linked to the ring by Cantrell some time before. They found him on November 29 to make the arrest.[206] Mason initially denied involvement but later admitted to resurrecting with Cantrell, West and Moffett to sell the corpses to Indiana Medical College.[207] Mason had been recruited by William Moffett several years prior when the two were drinking at an Indiana Avenue bar.

The following is Mason's statement as printed in the *Journal*:

> *I have known William Moffett for eight years. About six or seven years ago Moffett, Cantrell and myself went to the insane hospital[208] cemetery and got a body. We made two trips to this cemetery. One trip was a "water haul," as the body was gone when we opened the grave. The body that we got was delivered to the Indiana Medical College. It was taken to the rear*

*of the building and left on the inside of the floor. Moffett carried the body
into the building. I stayed in the buggy on the outside. Two or three days
after we delivered the body, Bill Moffett paid me $10 for my share for both
trips. The next trip, I think, we went to what is known as Round Point
Cemetery. Moffett and a colored man were with me. We got a body there
and delivered it to the Indiana Medical College. We put it on the floor of
the college the same as before. About two or three days afterward I got $5
for my share of the work. Moffett paid me. These trips were made about
four years ago. We used a two-seated wagon, Moffett always sat on the car
seat with the bodies.*[209]

Another farmer by the name of Henry Hartman visited Cantrell in jail
that November. Hartman wanted to know about graverobbing south of the
city, as he was of the mind that a fellow local farmer around his village
of Five Points was body snatching. Cantrell refused to disclose the name
but did share some relevant information. Hartman later told reporters that
he "expressed the sentiment of his section of the county as being in favor
of leniency to Cantrell. Without his information, the systematized grave
robbing would have continued indefinitely….for that reason his punishment
should be light."[210]

The month ended with Thanksgiving, and the jailed body snatchers were
treated to a holiday spread at the Marion County lockup.[211] The *Journal*
reported that at "the appointed hour the men were marched into the dining
room on the third floor, where they were confronted with heaped plates

Following is a tabulated record of arrests made and a monthly
statement of the value of stolen property recovered:

Murder	6
Gambling	24
Playing policy	36
Grand and petit larceny	319
Forgery	4
Embezzlement	20
Fugitives	72
Burglary	54
Highway robbery	11
Grave robbery	25
Miscellanous	312
Total	883

Mayor Bookwalter's report of arrests made in 1902. *From* The Journal Handbook of
Indianapolis, *Indianapolis–Marion County Public Library.*

of baked turkey, oyster dressing, mashed potatoes, cranberry sauce, celery, apples and bananas."[212]

Before the festivities began, Cantrell supposedly used his charismatic charm and penchant for preaching to make "a few remarks apropos of the day."[213] Cantrell sermonized on the biblical tale of the Return of the Prodigal Son. The "former preacher and self-confessed ghoul, then began a dissertation on the moral. His efforts at preaching were listened to attentively, and when he concluded by conferring benediction on the crowd, a loud hand-clapping was indulged in."[214]

CHAPTER 6

A FAMINE OF CADAVERS

Twenty-eight people were arrested in connection with body snatching and were awaiting prosecution that December, including Cantrell, James Harvey, Cassius Willis, Bud Richardson, William McElroy, Buford Cowley, Walter Daniels, Sol Grady, Sam Martin, Isom Donnell, Al Hunt and Garfield Buckner. Because of Cantrell's many disclosures, several other ghouls were on the docket, including Herman Fritz, Adam Ault, W.H. Spears, William Haymaker, William Jones, John McEndree, Hampton West, George Mason, Walter Williams, Leroy Williams and William Moffett. The list of physicians included Joseph Alexander, William Molt, Frank Wright, Charles Byrkit and J.C. Wilson.[215]

On December 1, Special Judge J.M. Bailey's criminal courtroom in the old 1876 Marion County Courthouse was packed with attorneys, physicians, medical students and a host of spectators. A pool of fifty jurors sat among the crowd, waiting for their turns to be interviewed.

Alexander "did not appear ill at ease," the *News* reported.[216] Indeed, he should have. The doctor faced "three indictments of three counts each for taking, concealing and buying human corpses," specifically the bodies of Rose Neidlinger, Glendora Gates and Stella Middleton.[217] As proceedings began, prosecutor Ruckelshaus filed a notice of *nolle prosequi*, seeking to drop the Neidlinger charges. The state had determined that Alexander could be indicted on a new charge for his involvement in the Neidlinger theft based on the discovery of laws that better matched Alexander's crime. Judge Bailey sustained the motion.

A typical circa 1900 medical college dissecting room. *Wellcome Collection.*

Sol Grady's mugshot photos from 1903. *Indiana State Archives.*

Prosecutors determined that Alexander violated two 1899 laws. The new charge "makes it necessary for the State to only prove that the body is in the possession of a medical college without the consent or permission of the nearest kin."[218] The laws, as written by the General Assembly, were as follows:

> *5620: Any person who shall dissect or have in his possession for the purpose of dissecting, any human body, or any part thereof, other than such as are or may be given by law to such uses, shall be deemed guilty of a felony, and upon conviction thereof, shall be imprisoned in the state prison for not less than two years nor more than five years.*[219]

> *5621: When such a body shall be received or found in any building or rooms of such school or college, or incorporated medical association, it shall, for the purpose of this act, or any prosecution thereunder, be deemed and taken to be in the possession of the person or persons who, under the rules of practice of such school or college or incorporated medical association, have the supervision of the dissecting room and the instruction given therein, unless the contrary be made to appear.*[220]

On the following day, the defense requested a delay in the proceedings so "that they should be allowed time in which to prepare…the additional count charged in the affidavit of information."[221] The prosecution challenged the motion, leading to a heated courtroom exchange. The "argument of the attorneys was spirited, and on several occasions, asides from the attorneys to each other indicated the keen fight that is to be made over the case."[222] Judge Bailey ruled for the defense and pushed the trial to December 15 in a "spirit of fairness."[223] The jury pool was dismissed.

Despite all of this, Indy's medical colleges still needed cadavers for their winter terms. The *Indianapolis News* reported on December 4 that "a famine of cadavers is feared by the authorities of medical colleges and as a consequence the price of bodies has advanced."[224] The colleges usually began each semester with about one hundred cadavers, but they had only about forty in December 1902.[225] Prior to Cantrell's arrest and the subsequent publicity, corpses fetched anywhere from five to ten dollars.[226] By December, however, dead bodies were going for fifty to seventy-five dollars.[227] The *News* reported "an extra fine 'subject' is worth $100."[228] It's not clear in the reports how the *News* obtained this information.

The paper concluded that the "scarcity is attributed to the Indianapolis investigation. It is said that ghouls in the employ of colleges all over

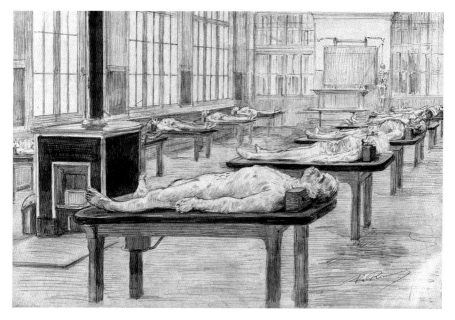

Interior of a dissecting room, by Paul Renouard (1906). *Wellcome Collection.*

the Central States have become apprehensive for fear that a general investigation be made and they are seeking other ways of earning a livelihood."[229] Rufus Cantrell, so it seemed, ushered in the decline of body snatching in central Indiana.

The resurrectionist resumed working with investigators in December. Whatever trepidations he had about working with prosecutors had apparently dissipated. Concerned members of the community also continued to seek Cantrell out for information. F.M. Hollingsworth and William Gulliver from Pike Township telephoned Cantrell to ask if any bodies had been taken from Bethel Cemetery. Rufus responded that "he was sorry to tell them that he thought every body buried in the place previous to the beginning of the investigation had been taken."[230]

Cantrell also admitted that he attempted to steal the body of William's father, Stephen Gulliver, but that a one-thousand-pound stone sat on top of the coffin. Cantrell's ghouls were unable to lift it and abandoned the effort. But on the next night, another crew of resurrectionists "lifted the stone and secured the body."[231]

Cantrell also offered information to assist in the arrest of one Lucius Stout, whom Cantrell identified as Hampton West's ghoulish sidekick.[232] It's not clear if Cantrell supplied the evidence for Stout's arrest or if he just corroborated it, but in either case, it was sufficient for deputy prosecutor Charles Benedict to submit it to a grand jury. During the interview that followed, Cantrell's attorney, Cass Connaway, asked the ghoul if he knew a man named Stout from Hamilton County. Rufus laughed and said he "guessed Connaway was referring to Lucius B. Stout, Hampton West's right bower."[233]

According to Cantrell, Stout was a farmer near Eagletown and stole bodies with West in Hamilton County, mostly around Westfield and Noblesville. Stout was even seen at several funerals of late, telling people that he was an undertaker's assistant. Cantrell admitted to grand jurors that he paid Stout for several bodies and that the Hamilton County ghoul also "acted as an agent and supplied information of the burials of persons who died in his neighborhood."[234]

Stout had made headlines earlier in the year due to his involvement in a bunco gambling case. His son was friends with a high school sprinter named Tyler Crothers. The younger Stout had bet on a race that Crothers was favored in, winning twenty-five dollars. Stout the elder, thinking of an easy payday, was convinced by Crothers to bet on a race he planned to throw in Illinois. "Crothers said he knew the ability of all the contestants in the race, and if Stout would bet his money…Crothers would fall."[235]

The cornpone ghoul then took out a $3,100 loan in his wife's name against the family farm. Crothers and Stout then traveled to Illinois via train for the fixed race. After securing bets, the competition began, but Crothers won! Stout "took the first train for home, and, after thinking over the matter several days, came to the conclusion that Crothers had entered into a conspiracy to defraud him."[236]

The naïve Stout was swindled. Crothers had actually devised the scheme with Horace Carey, the Hamilton County clerk. Casting pride to the wind, Stout pressed charges with the help of some Masonic friends. Crothers and Carey were arrested a few weeks later.[237]

IT'S HARD TO GAUGE contemporary public sentiment about all this. The case made headlines in the press almost daily that winter, but the papers don't write much about public opinion. We can assume, given the scope of the reporting, that Marion County residents were intrigued and following updates. At the end of the month, the *Noblesville Dispatch* reported that "the people of Hamilton county have been considerably wrought up over statements by Rufus Cantrell, that wholesale robberies of graves had occurred in that county."[238] The story continued to make national news.

Circa 1904 at Illinois and Washington Streets. *Library of Congress.*

As Alexander's case was set to begin mid-December, the doctor became conveniently ill. According to his physician, Frank Morrison, Alexander was suffering from walking typhoid fever.[239] The defense asked for another continuation, to which Judge Bailey agreed, setting the new trial date for January 12. A panel of jurors was released for a second time.[240]

Then something weird happened in an already bizarre story. Someone writing under the name of "Wallace Simms" began sending letters to IPD superintendent George Taffe. The notes disclosed information about Cantrell and the recent graverobberies. Simms accused the ghoul of stealing gold teeth from the bodies and selling the empty coffins to undertakers.[241]

In one letter postmarked from Louisville, Simms wrote that "one night, when Cantrell opened a grave, he found life yet in the body, and that Cantrell choked the man to death in order to sell the body."[242] Cantrell emphatically denied the accusation of murder, telling a reporter:

> *That's all foolishness. Anyone knows that a man would not live if plated under several feet of earth without air. That letter was written here in town with the objective of creating a sentiment against me. There was one short statement in one of the letters that no one except a certain doctor and myself know about. Either he or his attorney wrote the letter and signed it, Wallace Simms. I know every negro graverobber from Denver to New York, and there never was one by the name of Wallace Simms.*[243]

Cantrell believed that Dr. Frank Wright wrote the letter. When a *News* reporter asked Wright about the accusation, he said he didn't care what Rufus said, adding, "Let me tell you one thing, if that man Cantrell will tell what he knows about the right people, there will be a good many persons in trouble that are not involved so far."[244]

CHAPTER 7

THE STORY TURNS BIZARRE

A number of truly strange events occurred in January 1903 that turned this already peculiar story into a genuinely bizarre tale. Cass Connaway, Cantrell's lawyer, began the month by seeking a reduction in the ghoul's bail, which was now set at $2,000. Cantrell could not afford this. Connaway "thought that the State would be willing to lower his bond and might be induced to let Cantrell out on his own recognizance, providing someone would agree to keep a watchful eye on him."[245] In a hearing, prosecutor John Ruckelshaus countered that "it would be unwise and, inasmuch as Cantrell has lain in jail for some time, a continuance of his condition would not hurt him, while his liberation might be detrimental to the hopes of the State for a conviction of some of the prisoners."[246] Ruckelshaus also believed, with good reason, that "Cantrell might be approached and instructed in his testimony."[247] There was also a fear from the law enforcement that Rufus might skip town. Judge Alford denied Connaway's request in a sidebar.

Cantrell at this point became despondent and, as he had the previous November, refused to disclose any more information to investigators until his bail was reduced.[248] The *Indianapolis News* even printed a statement Cantrell released on January 7 indicating that he would no longer provide testimony to the grand jury or information to Asch and Manning. He apparently sent this without consulting Connaway, who was away on business. Cantrell also told reporters that "the influence of physicians was being exerted to get him to refuse to help the State."[249]

Left: John Ruckelshaus in 1912, Marion County prosecutor. *Library of Congress.*

Right: A poor rendering of Cantrell from the *New York Herald*, August 16, 1903. *Library of Congress.*

The newspaper reports about this differ in the details. It could've been bad journalism, or maybe Rufus told reporters different things. The press played a sizable role in the affair, and it's certainly possible that Cantrell actively sought to leverage the publicity to share his version of the summer of 1902. The *Indianapolis Journal* wrote on January 8 that "nearly every day Cantrell has asked to see one of the reporters from the daily papers. To one reporter he will confide that he is not being treated fairly in the matter and for the time the public will hear nothing more of grave robbing from him."[250] He told a reporter that the *Journal* "was the only paper in the city that had handled his case truthfully," but later told the *News* and the *Sentinel* the same thing.[251]

The mysterious "Wallace Simms" also continued his letter writing in early 1903. On January 7, Simms sent a note to police claiming to be an African American resurrectionist who had worked with Cantrell. The writer urged leniency for Dr. Alexander and Dr. Wright but not Rufus. The envelope had a Louisville postmark.[252]

The police rightly saw through this and were "of the opinion that Simms is a 'yellow journal' correspondent who is writing the letters at the dictation of one of the physicians under arrest."[253] Late in December, Simms also sent a letter to Chicago and New York newspapers suggesting that Cantrell had planned to steal the body of former president Benjamin Harrison from Crown

Hill Cemetery. The letter was published sensationally in yellow Chicago and New York newspapers. The Simms letter suggested that instead of selling the former president's body to a medical college, it would be ransomed back to the Harrison family. Then, "after the reward was offered [the body] was to be taken to the country and found by Cantrell, who would then claim the reward."[254] The idea was that Rufus would innocently stumble on the corpse and profit from "discovering" it.

Neither prosecutors nor the cops believed this. Rufus Cantrell, his fellow resurrectionists and the medical school doctors may have been immoral men, but they weren't stupid. Stealing an ex-president's body from a very well-guarded cemetery would have raised an enormous amount of attention. Simms's letter was then really only designed to provide false witness against Cantrell and raise public ire.

Interestingly, the body of Benjamin Harrison's father actually was snatched by resurrectionists and sold to a medical college twenty-three years prior. John Scott Harrison, the son of President William Henry Harrison and father of President Benjamin Harrison, had died in 1878; his body was interred in the family plot in North Bend, Ohio. His corpse was stolen by an Ohio ghoul named Charles Morton and sold to the Ohio Medical College in Cincinnati.[255] Incredibly, Harrison's son, John, had inadvertently discovered his dad's corpse when he was looking for *another* missing body, that of Augustus Devin. Devin's body was later discovered brining in a Michigan medical college vat, but John Scott Harrison's body was found by his son hanging from a rope down a shaft at Ohio Medical College.[256]

Hoosiers of a certain age would have remembered this story in 1903, as it was reported widely in papers across the United States. Nevertheless, Simms's incredulous accusations were rejected by IPD detectives as nonsense, even if the newspapers in New York and Chicago did not.

True or not, these letters disheartened Cantrell. Coupled with the court's unwillingness to lower his bail, he "sulked in his cell at the jail and every hour or two sends forth an edict that he will not aid the State in further investigation."[257] With his thick French accent, Detective Adolph Asch told a reporter that Cantrell was moody and "has a fit of melancholy every few days and he threatens to turn us down. He's all right now, however. He realizes that his only chance of having leniency shown to him is to continue to aid the State, and he is bright enough to do it."[258]

After Connaway returned, he met with his client and convinced Cantrell to continue working with prosecutors.[259] Rufus "admitted that several persons had been 'working' on him to 'stand pat' and not testify. He said he realized

Benjamin Harrison's funeral on March 17, 1901. *From* The Journal Handbook of Indianapolis, *Indianapolis–Marion County Public Library.*

that if he did not assist in the prosecution, he could expect no leniency in the disposition of his case."[260]

Cantrell demonstrated his "change of heart" by helping Asch and Manning secure yet another arrest. Early in January, "Captain Gerber and several of the other attaches of police headquarters have seen a strange man walking around the jail, as if trying to talk with someone near the barred windows."[261] The man in question was William A. Coffelt. The visitor hoped to speak with Cantrell, ostensibly to ask the ghoul if he knew any information about the body of Coffelt's aunt.[262]

Cantrell recognized the man, but not as William Coffelt. Rufus knew him as a fellow ghoul named Michael Foley. Cantrell had given Asch and Manning his name a few weeks back. Rufus told detectives that Foley was another leading graverobber, operating his own crew of white body snatchers in Greater Indianapolis, and was also once involved in a murder.[263]

Rufus refused to meet Coffelt initially but later decided to help detectives plan an ambush. When Coffelt returned in another attempt to chat, he was admitted and immediately began yelling at Cantrell. Rufus told the man to leave "or he would be arrested. Coffelt became angry and called Cantrell vile names."[264]

Coffelt was arrested and interrogated. Cantrell had said that Coffelt/ Foley was responsible for "stealing the bodies of Jonas Fertig from Eagle Creek Cemetery, Mrs. Cossell and John Harding from a cemetery west of Indianapolis, and a body from Fairview Cemetery, near the Belt road, on Pendleton Pike."[265] Coffelt was charged with the theft of all four bodies. During questioning:

> *Cantrell jumped from his chair and then asked Coffelt what had become of Billy Gray. "Is Billy Gray in Virginia or is he in heaven?" Cantrell asked Coffelt. The latter during the recital of the question hung his head, but when Cantrell finished, Coffelt raised his head and gave a mean look toward Cantrell. The latter continued: "You know who I mean; what about those bricks falling in the water one night after we left a certain cemetery?" Coffelt still refused to talk, and Cantrell laughed and shook his head knowingly.*[266]

The *News* also reported on the jailhouse interview. In its version, Cantrell asked Coffelt, "I suppose you know nothing of 'Big Blue.'"[267] Big Blue was the informal name body snatchers gave to a vacant parlay house "where the ghouls met to plan their expeditions and divide the territory."[268] The building sat opposite the old trolley car barns in Irvington. The area's graverobbers would assemble "there and at other places for a social time with a keg of beer."[269]

William Coffelt, aka Michael Foley, from the *Indianapolis News*, January 5, 1903. *Hoosier State Chronicles.*

When he wasn't stealing dead bodies, Coffelt worked as a machinist at Dean Pump Works. Two days before Christmas in 1898, Coffelt's fourteen-year-old son Frank died after accidentally falling into a vat of steam at the Indianapolis Basket Company.[270] The elder Coffelt attempted to sue a year later for $5,000 in damages. The outcome of the lawsuit isn't clear in the newspapers, but according to Cantrell, Coffelt attempted to sell his son's body to a medical college. This was a bridge too far even for Rufus Cantrell. The resurrectionist refused to buy and transfer it.[271]

During the interview, "Coffelt appeared dazed and he turned a deathly pallor."[272] His bail was set at $1,000, which he secured and was released.[273] A few days after Coffelt's arrest,

Cantrell appeared again before the grand jury to testify about Coffelt/Foley. The papers printed a rumor that Cantrell refused to cooperate, but this wasn't exactly true. Cantrell told a reporter, "I did not refuse to testify. I told the jurors that I was not ready to give my evidence against Coffelt, and then we spent the time discussing the grave robbing investigation in Hamilton county. One of the jurors lives near the county line, and he wanted my views on the matter and he got them."[274]

Just north of that line in Hamilton County, a warrant was issued on December 29, 1902, for Hampton West. The former Confederate was indicted with "stealing the bodies of Newton Bracken and Walter Manship from the Beaver cemetery, nine miles southeast of Noblesville. West is also under heavy bond to answer to two similar charges in Marion County."[275] Locals also accused West of "robbing the grave of his niece, Miss Ida West, the daughter of West's brother, William, who lives near Fisher's Station."[276]

The residents of Hamilton County despised Hamp. The *Hamilton County Ledger* reported on January 9 that "the feeling against West among the people in and about Fisher's Station is that of intense hatred, and a few boldly assert that unlawful punishment would be meted out to him if he escaped conviction in the courts."[277] Someone had already burned West's house down in early December. After the ghoul made bail the first time, he got a job at a livery stable but soon lost it when area farmers strong-armed the stable owner to fire him.[278]

A very nervous Hamp West sent a pleading letter to Cantrell in January 1903. West was being held in Noblesville and could not pay the $4,000 bail, and no one was willing to put up the necessary percentage to bond him out. The *News* reported, "West is breaking down under the strain of being confined."[279] The letter never reached Cantrell because it was either lost or stolen. But Hamp had dictated it to the Hamilton County sheriff, who later forwarded a copy to the *News*:

Mr. Cantrell—Dear Sir: I am in the Noblesville jail, charged with robbing graves. I am an old man, nearly broken down. Mr. Cantrell, you know you told me that you would not convict me, and now I want to know just what you are going to do. You have placed me in the position I am now in and I want to know what you will do. I never wanted to talk to a man as much as I do you. I want to talk with you, but my lawyers advise me not to. I am sorry I got as angry at you as I did, but when we meet again it will be different. You have done me more injury than any man you have implicated, and you will think so when you consider this matter. Mr. Cantrell, you think this thing over to the best advantage to both of us. The reason I write you is that I saw the article in the paper about Joe Alexander. I want you to consider his case of mine as I would consider your case if I were in your place. I read that you want to prepare to meet your God. Now, Mr. Cantrell, how can you do this if you convict me? Please answer by return mail.[280]

When reporters asked Cantrell about West's letter, he said he never received it. He supposedly told them:

State hasn't treated me right in anything, and I have no reason to be liberal with the information I have. West may be assured that I will do nothing to hurt his chances of liberty. He is an old man, and even though we have had some difficulties, I will hold no hate against him and will do all I can for the old man.[281]

I'm not entirely sure I believe this as published in the *News*. It's possible that Cantrell was in one of his moods; maybe he was still in a funk after the court refused to reduce bail. In any case, Cantrell eventually got West's letter and replied with a very different message:

Dear Sir—Your letter of January 9 received to-day. It found me well. In answer to your request that I refrain from convicting you. I will say that I intend to tell the truth. RUFUS CANTRELL[282]

Back in Indianapolis, Dr. Alexander's trial was slated to begin on January 12. But the doctor was still "suffering" from typhoid. The court was suspicious and subpoenaed Alexander's physician, Frank Morrison, to confirm, but he never showed. Morrison later gave the excuse that the subpoena never came. Judge Bailey reluctantly granted a third continuance, pushing Alexander's trial to Groundhog Day. Bailey also limited the courtroom audience to reporters and "those directly interested in the case."[283]

The delays began to irritate prosecutors, who saw through to what was really going on.[284] When Morrison showed at a second hearing, Ruckelshaus asked the court to appoint its own physician to examine Alexander, but Judge Bailey denied the request.[285] Judge Alford, though not presiding over the case, also found the delays irksome. He told the *Journal*, "Like General Grant, they would fight it out in that line if it took all summer. There will be no adjournment of this court until after Alexander is brought to trial. No summer vacation for myself or the prosecutor until the docket is cleared of the grave robbing cases."[286]

Toward the end of the month, an unsigned letter was sent to Superintendent Taffe and to the *Indianapolis News*. The letter said that a few Indy police officers had stopped Cantrell one night during a graverobbing excursion some years prior. The ghoul supposedly paid the cops five dollars each to let him go. These officers were, according to the letter, still patrolling at Howland Station, "near the end of College avenue."[287] It's not clear if anything came from this, but Cantrell refused to discuss the letter.

Then something profoundly bizarre and intensely stupid happened, like a scene out of a campy 1960s sitcom. Sheriff Metzger intercepted a package at the jail addressed to Cantrell. Its contents included a saw and metal files, gifted ostensibly so Cantrell could cut his way out from behind bars. Metzger laughed it off, telling a reporter, "It's only a foolish scheme. Anyone knows that a box would be opened before it is delivered to the prisoners."[288] The package had a New Albany postmark.

No one took it seriously, especially seeing how Rufus never made any attempt to escape. Despite his occasional moodiness, Cantrell was generally cooperative during the investigation. He also could have attempted to run during any of the cemetery fact-finding missions but didn't. A nail file in a box? Come on. This seems stupid even for 1902. Maybe the point was to make the whole thing a farce.

Cantrell didn't find it funny. He was furious. He declared that "he would remain silent no longer and that he would give information that would lead to many arrests. He accuses Dr. F.M. Wright, who is under indictment, with perpetrating the scheme. [Cantrell] said he and Dr. Wright had made several visits to New Albany together, and that the physician had friends in a certain undertaking establishment in that city and a physician in Louisville, who assisted him in former deals."[289]

Cantrell, like his Hamilton County counterpart Hampton West, also began breaking under the strain of confinement. He told reporters in late January that he really wanted out of jail, as did his fellow graverobbers who also couldn't afford bail. Cantrell attempted to appeal to the city's Black community for aid. He wrote a letter to Reverend Benjamin Farrel of the Mount Zion Baptist Church, a congregation where Rufus once preached, asking for help:

> *Sir, I want to appeal to your people that I am the victim of one of the strongest and powerful race that is upon the face of the globe, which they*

are coming to the rescue of one that is in trouble. Sir, while I am on the other side I can call four or five of our race leaders who are doing all in their power to aid the white man and are trying to convict us poor-colored boys, who are in jail, and God knows that we alone are not to blame. Sir, I will say to you among these colored race leaders one of them is one of the leading doctors in this city. So, as I write you this letter I shall do the same to all of the colored churches in this city, as I am a prisoner I can only appeal to the churches as I think the honorable part of my race are there. I believe that you know, dear elder, that I once was a God-fearing man, but after I commenced to lead a fast life and this is where I landed. So I can only think of your kind teaching that you have so often told me through your sermons, which was "your sins will find you out," but after I had fell in the hands of justice, dear sir, I only remember another part of your dear words, which are, "An open confession is good for the soul." Dear sir, after my little trouble with the church, I only felt as an outcast and went backward in serving my Maker. I can say to you that the State never was sincere in the prosecution of the case, and the only hope for me is to wear me out in jail. If something is not done for me I may have to lay in jail for two or three years and then go to the State prison for ten years. I hope that you will let me know by return mail what steps you will take in trying to aid me. I have told nothing but the truth in the whole matter.[290]

Reverend Farrell refused, telling the *News*:

I am not in sympathy with crime or criminals. This man Cantrell deserves no sympathy, and is, according to his own confession, a heartless type of criminal. I would not succeed, either, with my people, who knew Cantrell well before he was ex-communicated from this church for unchristian conduct and I would not humiliate myself in their estimation by making such an appeal to them.[291]

Cantrell's requests to other Indy-area African American churches met similar responses. The *Indianapolis Recorder*, Indiana's leading Black weekly newspaper, openly criticized Cantrell's call for aid on January 31: "Rufus Cantrell, King of Ghouls, has directed an appeal for aid to the colored citizens through the Rev. B.F. Farrell. His request has been rudely and firmly declined. It was an insult to the race."[292]

The *Recorder* doubled down the next week:

We still insist that his request for aid was an insult. Why should the
colored people compromise with crimes or criminals, by furnishing aid to
the guilty? The sentiment of this community is that no guilty man white or
black should escape and we believe that Cantrell by his stated evidence, has
commended his punishment to the mercy of the court. It is the effort of the
race to encourage a better citizenship, and not a criminal one.[293]

Members of Indy's Black community, like most of the rest of the city, were
disgusted at the whole affair and found *all* graverobbers to be immoral men.
Out of options, Cantrell asked Detectives Asch and Manning for an escort
to a photography studio so he could have his portrait taken. He intended to
sell copies to raise money for his release.[294]

It's not always clear what truly persuaded Rufus Cantrell to cooperate
as he did, but earlier in the month, he supposedly told a *Journal* reporter
another bizarre tale that, if true, provided a motivation for Cantrell to seek
an end to the summer's orgy of graverobbing:

While Cantrell was discussing the arrest of Coffelt, he told of the finding
of Stella Middleton's body and the beginning of the grave-robbing expose.
He said he and the girl had been sweethearts, but two weeks before her

A 1902 photo of South Meridian Street. *From* The Journal Handbook of Indianapolis,
Indianapolis–Marion County Public Library.

death, he had occasion to leave the city and had gone to Orange county. Before leaving, the girl asked him if she could write to him while he was away. Cantrell said he would not allow her to write to him as he would be located in such out-of-the-way places that if he corresponded with anyone the letters might not reach him and some day they might be detrimental to him. When he left the city Miss Middleton was in good health. Two weeks later when he returned he was astounded to learn that the girl had died. He said he did not learn where she was buried, but the next night after the burial he, in company with two other ghouls, went to the old Anderson cemetery to rob a grave. Cantrell said it was a dark night and he did not notice the features of the corpse until the Central Medical College was reached. Then for the first time he weakened, he said, and could not carry the body into the cellar. His spirits were depressed, he said, and after the girl's body had been deposited in a barrel he resolved to have it returned to the grave. It was then he said that he went to Mrs. Middleton's house one rainy night and left the note telling her where the body of her daughter could be found. Cantrell said that after the body had been replaced in the grave he had the hardest time to keep the gang of ghouls from again stealing it.[295]

CHAPTER 8

DEPOPULATING CITIES
OF THE DEAD

Alexander's Trial, Part I

D r. Joseph Alexander's trial finally got underway on Groundhog Day in 1903. Court proceedings began promptly at 9:00 a.m. The case was called to trial as no. 33647. Alexander was up against four counts: "taking a corpse from a grave; concealing the body; buying a corpse, knowing it to be stolen, and having in his possession a stolen body."[296]

The defense began with two motions: the first to move forward on only one of four counts, under the idea that each count required a separate trial. The second motion was for dismissal, arguing that the original indictment was faulty. The state countered that all four counts were for the same crime, just different phases of one felony. Judge Bailey overruled both defense motions, reserving "the right to have the State elect one count if the evidence submitted to the jury was justified."[297]

The thirty-eight-year-old Dr. Alexander arrived at the courthouse "pale and evidently not enjoying the best of health."[298] He was seated with his new defense team: John Spahr, Martin Hugg and Henry Spaan. Across the aisle sat the state's attorneys, Marion County prosecutor John Ruckelshaus and his deputies, William Brown and Charles Benedict.

The first day of the trial was spent grilling potential jurors from a venire of seventy Marion County residents. The *News* reported that the defense was striking any candidate who was a farmer under the idea that most of the graverobbing occurred in rural cemeteries. The day ended without a full twelve.

William Brown in 1912, deputy prosecutor. *Library of Congress*.

The next day began with prosecutors excusing several potential jurors who had personal connections to Alexander or one of the other ghoulish doctors. By day's end, however, both sides had agreed on twelve jurors: Timothy Hussey, a contractor from Washington Township; Stephen Cook, a retired farmer from Indy; Harry Davis, an Indianapolis plumber; William Lister, an Indy stockbroker; R.W. Lingengelter, a clerk at Foster Lumber; T.W. Brown, an Indianapolis bookkeeper; H.A. Hickman, owner of the Rockwood Manufacturing Company; Charles Faulkner, the president of the Faulkner-Webb pickle company; James White, a cigar salesman on Market Street; John Pasquier, a carpenter; Joseph Theasing, a farmer from Decatur Township; and William Gimble, a paper salesman from Indianapolis.[299]

In an attempt to keep the jurors away from the growing media circus surrounding the trial, Judge Bailey ordered Alexander's peers to live together at the Marion County Courthouse. They were given cots to sleep on.[300]

Later in the day, the *News* reported the sensational story that the *Journal* had published early about Cantrell inadvertently resurrecting and selling the body of his dead girlfriend, Stella Middleton. The *News* told readers that Rufus "may repeat to the Criminal Court jury trying Dr. Joseph Alexander, the story he told the grand jury of the night he determined to wash his hands of the graverobbing business, and do all in his power to rectify the wrong he had done the relatives of the dead."[301] The *News* informed readers that the "story of the shock he experienced when he realized that his outrageous trafficking in human bodies had led him to despoil the grave of the only woman he cared for, Stella Middleton."[302]

Charles Benedict delivered the state's opening statement the following morning. Benedict told the jury that the Indiana General Assembly "provided strong penalties for demonstrators getting bodies unlawfully. Even for the crime of having in his possession a body that had been stolen from the grave or obtained in any manner other than those prescribed by the statutes, they fixed a penalty of from two to five years imprisonment."[303] Benedict furthered that the state will "show you that there was between Dr. Alexander and Rufus Cantrell a contract, agreement and understanding, which Cantrell was to obtain material for the college for the season. He was

THE JURY IN THE ALEXANDER CASE.

W. H. GIMBLE.   JOHN B. PASQUIRE.   STEPHEN COOK.   JNO. MENDENHALL, Bailiff.
ROBT. F. LINGENFELTER.   CHAS. F. FAULKNER.
H. A. EICKMAN.   JAMES O. WHITE.   TIMOTHY HUSSEY.   HARRY L. DAVIS.   JOSEPH TEASING.   T. W. BROWN.   W. J. LISTER.

Alexander's jury, from the *Indianapolis News*, February 5, 1903. *Hoosier State Chronicles.*

to get twenty or thirty bodies and Dr. Alexander agreed to pay him for his dirty work the sum of $20 a body."[304]

Benedict laid out the ring's inner workings, as orchestrated by the doctor:

> *Alexander was to do his part by going to the Board of Health. And he did his work, we shall show by the Health Board officers, by making daily visits to the board's office, searching the death returns and burial permits and getting lists of the newly-buried, whose grave he wished outraged. We shall show that under this contract, Cantrell and Martin and Sol Grady and others of the hideous band were paid from $3 to $5 each for their nights work.*[305]

Benedict also told jurors that the state would prove that the bodies of Glendora Gates, Wallace Johnson and Rose Neidlinger were all taken to Central College of Physicians and Surgeons—"according to the contract, Cantrell and his gang put a number of bodies into the Central College." Prosecutors endeavored "to prove by Cantrell that Stella Middleton's body was taken there, and by Justice of the Peace Nickerson that it was still there when he entered the college under a search warrant."[306]

He also described witnesses the state intended to call, including several ghouls who "made repeated trips to Dr. Alexander's office in the Claypool Building, and with him planned the graveyard raids, and that he paid them money from time to time."[307]

Benedict closed:

> *The State will insist that the evidence surrounding the Hotel de Hoss, the livery barn from which the gang always started, where it hired rigs for this nefarious work—those rigs paid for by Dr. Alexander—and where Dr. Alexander was seen repeatedly in their company, both day and night, shows conclusively that there was a systematic arrangement on the part of Dr. Alexander and Rufus Cantrell to fill the college vats with material by depopulating the cities of the dead on the country hillsides of Marion County.*[308]

Alexander sat calmly through these proceedings, although "not nearly so pale as on Monday and showed his interest in the trial."[309] The *News* wrote, "Dr. Alexander did not show any signs of mental uneasiness, and he calmly glanced about the room."[310] Alexander's wife, Julia, was also in the courtroom and described by the *News*:

> *Mrs. Alexander is a pretty and well dressed woman about thirty years old. She was attired in a black-made dress with a black boa about her neck, and she wore a black hat of medium size, trimmed with black ostrich plumes. She also wore eyeglasses with gold rims. She did not seem to be perturbed although she glanced frequently at her husband who consulted in whispers with his attorneys.*[311]

Henry Spaan in 1897, one of Dr. Alexander's lawyers. *Library of Congress.*

Before testimony began, Alexander's attorney, Henry Spaan, asked Judge Bailey to separate the ghouls currently held in jail so they couldn't coordinate testimony. Bailey agreed and ordered Cantrell's crew divided.

Prosecutors called Manson Neidlinger to the stand first. The grieving husband recounted his tale, including the mysterious phone call that led to the discovery of his wife's pickled body at Central College.

Cantrell was next, having arrived at court midmorning. Rufus was dressed in a "new suit of clothes and overcoat, in his small bow tie sparkled a cluster of brilliants that would have stocked a small jewelry store. Before leaving the jail, Cantrell made the request that no strangers be allowed to come close to him. He laughingly remarked that someone might stick something in him."[312]

Whatever confidence he had faded by the time he took his oath: "Cantrell showed decided signs of uneasiness. He seemingly had lost much of his bluff manner and confidence, as all the questions put to him were answered in a quiet manner."[313] Cantrell's attorney, Cass Connaway, encouraged his client to be brave and impressed on him "the importance of keeping his wits about him and not taking offense at any of the questions asked of him."[314]

The prosecution began by asking Rufus about body snatching, including questions regarding thefts not germane to Alexander's case. Defense attorney Henry Spaan objected, arguing that the testimony about bodies not listed in Alexander's indictment would confuse jurors. Judge Bailey briefly dismissed the jury to discuss. Brown countered that "in order to show guilty knowledge, motive and intent, the State had a right to produce evidence of other crimes. The State had already shown [Alexander] or the college in possession of nine bodies"[315] and that the state was able to "show that the doctor was instrumental in having from ten to seventeen graves robbed and a number of these bodies taken to the college."[316] Bailey overruled Spaan's objection. The jury was brought back in, and Cantrell's questioning resumed.

CHIEF WITNESS AGAINST DR. ALEXANDER.

RUFUS CANTRELL,
Whose Confession Resulted in Unearthing the Traffic in Stolen Bodies Carried on in Indianapolis.

The ghoul testified that he was originally from Gallatin, Tennessee, and had lived in Indianapolis for about ten years.[317] He first met Alexander in June 1902 at the latter's office in the Newton Claypool Building. Ruckelshaus asked the ghoul, "What did Dr. Alexander say to you?"[318]

Rufus responded, "He wanted to make a contract with me to furnish dissecting material for the college. I told him I had quit the business and only wanted to work in the college. He told me if I would work for him he would pay me the top price, and, besides, help me out at the college."

Cantrell on his way to testify in Alexander's trial, from the *Indianapolis News*, February 4, 1903. *Hoosier State Chronicles.*

Alexander offered thirty dollars per body. Cantrell agreed to the scheme on the condition that the doctor provide some of the tools. The ghoul bought a brace and a bit, while Alexander provided shovels and four revolvers he obtained from a pawnbroker on Indiana Avenue.

The next day, according to Cantrell, he went with Dr. Alexander to the courthouse, as the latter retrieved a list of the recently deceased from the Board of Health.

"What did he say to you?" Ruckelshaus asked.

"He said he had a good many places on his list. One of them was at Longwood, I remember. All of them were out of the county. There was work in Danville, and he wanted to know if I could work there. When I said I could, he gave me $3 to go there and look over the ground. I went there and saw Dr. Farrabee. I found the place could be easily worked and I returned and reported to Dr. Alexander."

The defense objected, saying that the activity in Danville was out of Marion County's jurisdiction. Judge Bailey sustained the motion. After some arguments regarding evidence, court was adjourned for lunch.

Rufus continued after the break, admitting to the theft of Meredith McMullen's body at Lick Creek Cemetery. McMullen's sister was in the courtroom that day and "was much affected. The graves of two of her brothers had been robbed."[319]

Cantrell admitted that he stole the body of Glendora Gates, the woman whose corpse was found in a sack that previous October. The defense objected and demanded a date, to which Cantrell replied without missing a beat, "July 10, 1902." He had been paid thirty dollars for the Gates body by Alexander.

Cantrell also admitted to resurrecting the bodies of Johanna Stilz, Wallace Johnson, Rose Neidlinger, Stella Middleton, Catherine Greene, Catherine Doehring and three others from the Central State Hospital. Alexander only gave him twenty dollars for the body of Wallace Johnson, who had been killed by a train, because "his body was badly mangled."[320] Cantrell recalled that Stilz was taken from Ebenezer Cemetery, Doehring from the German Catholic Cemetery and Middleton from the Anderson Cemetery. All bodies were delivered to the Central College of Physicians and Surgeons.

Rufus was "asked about Stella Middleton, who has been called Cantrell's sweetheart. Cantrell talked reticently of his theft of her body. He said that it was because he unknowingly robbed her grave that he notified her family. He said nothing about being her sweetheart."[321]

He told the jury, "I was paid for my services by Dr. Alexander. He made a payment on a diamond ring for me and got my clothes out of pawn. He bought me shoes and hired a rig for me."[322]

The defense continued cross-examination the next day, with questioning led by Henry Spaan. Bailey ordered the packed courtroom to be absolutely silent during proceedings. As for Cantrell, his "sulky and insolent manner of evading questions and volunteering unsought information was criticized sharply by Judge Bailey."[323]

Spaan asked about the Hotel de Hoss, the livery where Cantrell and his gang hired horses, carts and rigs from Douglas Case, the proprietor.[324] Cantrell said that the rigs were paid for by Joseph Alexander to haul tools and resurrectionists to cemeteries and bodies back to medical colleges. Spaan accused Cantrell of charging Alexander for additional excursions so that he could acquire bodies for other colleges. Rufus denied this and said the real reason he took out other rigs was to ferry his girlfriends about town on dates. The courtroom erupted in laughter. The ghoul also admitted to working out a scam to overcharge Alexander for each rental, with Case and Cantrell splitting the difference.[325]

Some of his answers during this round of questioning "did not please the State's lawyers, who noticed that while the audience laughed at some of the remarks the witness made, the members of the jury did not appear to grasp the humor of the situation."[326]

The defense made an attempt "to get Cantrell to admit that the story recently printed in an evening paper to the effect that he had been diverted from his purpose of robbing a grave by a discovery of his sweetheart in the grave, was false, but objections by Prosecutor Ruckelshaus barred the testimony."[327]

After being asked again about his criminal record, Cantrell admitted to being arrested three or four times, twice for assault and battery. On one occasion, Alexander even paid the fine.[328]

Spaan asked, "Weren't you arrested for embezzling money from the Zion Church?"

"I was."

"Didn't you shoot a man five times in a saloon?"

"I did."

Rufus also answered questions about his professional and personal life, stating that he had worked at the Post-Graduate College in Chicago, but only to assist the doctors in dissection, not as a body snatcher. He was married in Tennessee and had a child but "had not seen his wife since a short time before he was arrested." She lived in Louisville.[329]

Cantrell said he was twenty-three years old and had left Tennessee for Indianapolis with his family in 1893. He also testified that he had been employed as a night watchman at the Big Four coal yard but was fired for dishonesty.[330] Spaan then accused Cantrell of pawning several guns that Alexander had purchased for him. The ghoul admitted to this and to threatening Gus Habich's clerk, the gunsmith who had sold Cantrell guns on credit.

At one point during questioning, Spaan asked, "Mr. Cantrell, are you a Christian?"

Rufus responded that he was indeed a believer, although he denied giving the jailhouse sermon on Thanksgiving last. He told the jury that for about eight years, he'd been moonlighting at the pulpit, having first preached in Pewee Valley, Kentucky, and later at Mount Zion Baptist in Indy. He identified himself as "an itinerant preacher and had robbed graves during his pulpit service."[331]

When asked about his entry into graverobbing, Cantrell replied:

> *I don't remember when I robbed my first grave, but it was about six years ago, in the Lick Creek Cemetery, I think. I robbed three or four graves during that winter. I rested for two or three years, but about two years ago took to robbing graves again. I took bodies from graves in this and other counties. I have never called myself the "king of the ghouls," nor signed myself to that title in letters to newspapers. I have been known as the king of the ghouls for two or three years, and was first called that by physicians who employed me.[332]*

Henry Spaan in 1912, one of Alexander's lawyers. *Library of Congress.*

Spaan also attempted to discredit Cantrell by linking him to the recent murder. In early May 1902, a Chinese immigrant named Dong Gang Tshun (named in the press "Doc Lung") was killed in his laundry facility in the Shiel Building on Indiana Avenue. Lung's head was almost entirely severed from his neck. The brutal murder attracted a great deal of attention but also outrage from the city's Chinese immigrant community. A man by the name of Doc Gung Thee was arrested for the killing but was later exonerated in light of little evidence.

Cantrell replied that he knew nothing personally about the murder and that everything he knew, he learned from Dr. Frank Wright at the Eclectic Medical College. Spaan told the jury that he asked about Lung because he believed Cantrell had "telephoned Dr. Wright and asked him if he wanted to use the body of a Chinese for the purpose of dissection."[333]

Cantrell again denied knowing anything about Doc Lung's murder and repeated that Dr. Wright was the one to ask about Lung's murder. Spaan changed the subject: "While you were robbing graves and furnishing bodies to the Central College, you were furnishing bodies to other places, weren't you?"

Ruckelshaus objected but was overruled. Cantrell answered that he did not furnish any bodies to the other medical colleges. When asked about his fellow ghouls, he answered that he had worked with Sam Martin, Walter Daniels, William Jones, Leroy Williams, Walter Williams, Isom Donnell and Buford Cowley.

The defense also tried to discredit Cantrell by calling into question his mental stability. Spaan asked, "Were you ever discharged from the army for insanity or other cause similar to insanity?"

"No, sir."

"Were you discharged for epilepsy?"

"No sir. I don't know what epilepsy is. I am not very well educated and if you explain what it means I may be able to answer you."

"Do you know what insanity is? Don't you know whether you were discharged for insanity or not?"

"No, sir."

In dramatic fashion, Spaan pulled out and read a letter from the War Department, signed by Major General Corbin, adjutant general of the U.S. Army. The letter showed that

> *Private Rufus Cantrell, who had enlisted in Indianapolis on Nov. 12, 1897, to serve three years, had been discharged from Company A. Twenty-fourth United States Infantry, at Fort Douglas, Utah, on March 13, 1898, on a surgeon's certificate of disability. The cause of the disability was stated as "epilepsy, followed by confusional and suicidal insanity."*[334]

Ruckelshaus objected but was again overruled. The *Journal* speculated that Rufus faked poor mental health to get out of duty. Even if this was true, it didn't help Cantrell's credibility.

The ghoul was dismissed after the theatrics, and Sol Grady was called next to the stand. Grady testified that he had known Cantrell for seven years and that "he visited Anderson and Ebenezer cemeteries, and had stolen corpses in company with Cantrell and the others."[335]

Isom Donnell's mugshot photo from 1903. *Indiana State Archives*.

Isom Donnell, Cantrell's cousin, testified next that he had robbed the graves of Rose Neidlinger and Stella Middleton with Rufus. Donnell's wife had died sometime before, and Spaan accused the ghoul of selling her body for dissection, asking, "Isn't it a fact that you remained away from the funeral because of an agreement between you, the undertaker, and Cantrell to take your wife's body to a medical college."

"No, sir," replied Donnell.

Ruckelshaus then called William Jones, who testified that he had known Cantrell for four years. He told the jury that Alexander was present at Anderson Cemetery when the resurrectionists stole the body of Glendora Gates. He confirmed that the nightly excursions always started at Hotel de Hoss.

The courtroom was again jammed with spectators the next day. In melodramatic fashion, the state began by entering the burial shroud of Catherine Doehring into evidence, grandly displaying it for all to see. Phoebe Mock was called to testify, as she had dressed Doehring before burial. The silken shroud, with a very dead Catherine in it, had been found in a sack one misty October morning outside of Central College.

Catherine's daughter then took the stand. She "excited the sympathy of the auditors who heard her tearfully relate the circumstances of her mother's burial and later sorrowfully identified the stained garment as the shroud she had sewn together for her mother's lifeless body."[336] Soft tears were no doubt shed among those witnessing such high drama in court that day.

The prosecutors followed by calling a series of witnesses in rapid succession, including Dr. J.F. Barnill, the secretary of the faculty at Central College; M.E. Donelly, a reporter for the *Journal*; E.R. Gates, Glendora's brother; George Stilz, grandson of Johanna; Frank Duncan, police officer; Frank Doehring, son of Catherine; Sam Martin and Walter Daniels, ghouls; Douglas Case, Hotel de Hoss proprietor; Oral Miller, bookkeeper for the W.R. Bear Installment Firm; Arthur McKee, gunsmith assistant to Gus Habich; William Nickerson, justice of the peace; Frank Jones and John Barnett, Hotel de Hoss employees; Herb Green, a clerk at the Marion County Board of Health Office; and W.A. Rustin, embalmer.[337]

Most of the testimony served to establish and corroborate mundane facts. Walter Daniels, a graduate of the Tuskegee Institute, testified that he only participated in one body snatching excursion when the ghouls went after Stella Middleton's body. He told the jury that he was paid three dollars for his work and that Alexander was at the cemetery that night.

On Saturday morning, the defense tried again to limit the number of counts against Alexander. Hugg made a motion "that the four counts against Alexander…each constituted a distinct offense and should be tried separately." Judge Bailey denied the motion. Court adjourned when the state rested its case against Dr. Joseph Alexander.

CHAPTER 9

YOUR WIFE IN A PICKLING VAT

Alexander's Trial, Part II

On Monday morning, February 9, 1903, Alexander's lawyers began their opening statements. The defense used several tactics in an attempt to secure an acquittal, including racism. Spaan told the jury that "Dr. Alexander was of good moral character and stood well in the community for truth and veracity, while the negroes who testified against him were disreputable and unworthy of belief."[338] The defense also argued that while Alexander did, in fact, hire Cantrell to deliver bodies, he did so with the understanding that Rufus would obtain them legally.

Alexander's lawyers also maintained that the doctor never went body snatching with the ghouls and that his daily trips to the Board of Health were just a routine part of his job. The defense also claimed that Cantrell was being bribed to give false testimony. Spaan intended to "show that Cantrell had received $55" in a plain white envelope "with no signature and the address printed in a disguised hand."[339]

He also told jurors that Cantrell was insane, given his discharge due to "epilepsy, followed by confusional and suicidal insanity." The defense also planned to showcase Cantrell's immorality by introducing "expert testimony to show that a man afflicted as Cantrell was—as shown by his discharge from the regular army—a moral monster and has no conception of right and wrong."[340]

Spaan concluded his remarks by tugging on the jury's heartstrings:

Joseph Alexander and his wife leaving the Marion County Courthouse in February 1903. *Indiana State Library.*

Once while Mr. Spaan, in a pathetic voice, told the life history of Dr. Alexander, relating how he had begun at the very lowest rung of the ladder, sunk in the deepest poverty, the tears coursed down Dr. Alexander's face, and all over the room men and women were putting handkerchiefs to their eyes. The jury for the first time seemed affected.[341]

What the *News* didn't report on was just how far the prosecutors' eyes must have been rolling back into their heads. Deputy prosecutor William Brown objected once during the charade, although he was overruled. The attorneys bickered constantly as the morning advanced, so much so that Bailey called a sidebar, telling both that "this is not a contest of lawyers and if we get off your feet once in a while, I hope the jury will pardon us."[342]

Spaan's opening statement lasted two hours and forty-five minutes. After a lunch recess, court resumed with character witnesses who testified about Dr. Alexander's supposed moral faculty. William S. Overstreet, cousin to Congressman Jesse Overstreet, testified on behalf of Alexander's incorruptible character. Overstreet's assessment of the doctor was supported by Edgar Wilson, an Indy druggist; Walter Ballart, president of the Abbatoir

William Brown in 1897, deputy prosecutor. *Library of Congress.*

Company of Indianapolis; F.W. Samuels, manager at the Postal Telegraph Company; Ferdinand Mueller, another Indy druggist; City Councilman John Crall; Charles Lavery, a cigar dealer; Herman Tombs, pharmacist; Charles Gregg, engineer; Edward Moffatt, doctor; Herman Fowler, druggist; E.R. Monroe, real estate agent; Joseph Kepler, manager of R.G. Dunn and Company; Frank Rupert, furniture dealer; John Weaver, lawyer; Harry Zimmer, druggist; and J.M. LaFollette, deputy district attorney. All spoke of Alexander's sterling character.[343] E.G. Groenwoldt, the doctor's brother-in-law, testified that he and Alexander rented a rig from Hotel de Hoss for a medical trip one evening, certainly not to snatch dead bodies.

The defense also called several "specialists" to answer questions about Cantrell's mental health, none of whom, mind you, actually examined the ghoul. Over an objection from prosecutors, Dr. W.B. Fletcher took the stand first. Spaan bluntly asked him if he thought Rufus was sane or insane. Fletcher responded, "He is insane without a doubt."[344] Under cross, Fletcher admitted to formerly working at Central College and knowing the doctors under indictment. Dr. Charles White and E.C. Reyer, a doctor at the Central Indiana Hospital for the Insane, testified similarly. Reyer told the jury that Cantrell "may be morally defective and still able mentally. I would call the case one of moral imbecility."[345] The defense also put on the stand Dr. H.M. Lash, a specialist from the Athens Lunatic Asylum in Ohio. He told the jury that he considered Rufus "the man of one unsound mind."[346]

Witness testimony continued into the following day. The courtroom was again full, filled with all manner of interested parties—even the "galleries and other reserved places were filled with women, many of them well dressed and all intensely interested."[347] Midmorning, Alexander took the stand in his own defense. The *News* wrote that the doctor "appeared pale, but not ill at ease and he spoke in a low clear tone. The dark rings under his eyes showed the effects of the strain under which he has been during the trial."[348]

The ghoulish doctor calmly answered his lawyer's questions. He testified that "he was a self-made man. He was born thirty-eight years ago in Hamilton county, and was left an orphan when a child."[349] He was raised by his grandparents and worked as a blacksmith and a druggist before moving to Indy to become a doctor. He had graduated from Indiana University in 1895 and opened a general practice on South Noble Street. Two years later, he moved into the Newton Claypool Building. In 1901, he was hired under contract with Central College to deliver thirty lectures per semester on osteology. After a successful year, he was appointed as the director of the anatomical laboratory at the school. His duties included demonstrating dissections for students and securing cadavers. It cost the doctor "in time, labor and money, about $12.50 to preserve a body and place it in a barrel of brine."[350] Alexander said the school needed about ten to fifteen bodies each semester, given the current demand of enrolled students.

Character sketch of Dr. Alexander, from the *Indianapolis News*, February 13, 1903. *Hoosier State Chronicles.*

Alexander added that he hired Cantrell to clean the school's existing skeletons in June 1902 and then contracted with him to deliver cadavers later that summer. He denied buying Rufus shovels and going with him to dig up bodies. He claimed no foreknowledge about Cantrell's previous graverobbing activities when he hired the ghoul.

Spaan concluded by asking the doctor, "Did you know that he was getting bodies illegally?"

"No, sir," replied the doctor. Alexander added that Cantrell fulfilled the order in late summer with what he believed were legally obtained corpses. He reiterated that he made no attempt to hide cadavers during the autumn searches.

During cross, Brown asked Alexander, "Did you not ask any questions about these bodies?"

"No, I did not," Alexander replied.

Brown was deputized to help prosecutors, from the *Indianapolis News*, February 13, 1903. *Hoosier State Chronicles.*

Brown turned on his heel to the jury to proclaim, "I want to show that this witness is so reckless that he did not care where these bodies came from. He admitted that he did not know where they came from."[351]

Some of Brown's questions turned macabre. "When you were preparing the bodies for the pickle, did you remove the hair?"

"Sometimes," said Alexander.

"Did you remove the hair from the Neidlinger body?"

"I don't remember."

The doctor was dismissed, and the defense next called his wife, Julia. Her entrance caused "a stir in the large crowd in the court-room, which tried to get a glimpse of her."[352] Julia, "dressed in a neat-fitting tailor-made gown of black, walked to the witness chair and was sworn to testify in her husband's behalf."[353] On the stand, she waxed poetic on her husband's oozing moral fortitude.

Mrs. Alexander was dismissed, and the defense rested. The prosecution then called a few rebuttal witnesses, including John Comer, an ex-deputy sheriff, who testified that Cantrell was quite sane, given his daily interactions with the ghoul. W.J. Schleicher, the grand jury foreman who had interviewed Cantrell multiple times, also testified that Cantrell was lucid and mentally stable. Sheriff Robert Metzger said the same, as did *Journal* reporter Michael Donelly.[354]

Before the next morning's proceedings got underway, the defense moved "that all the evidence be withdrawn from the jury which tended to show the bodies of Mrs. Stilz, Estelle Middleton, Glendora Gates, Mrs. Doehring, Catherine Green, Meredith McMullen and three bodies from the graveyard of the Insane Asylum."[355]

Judge Bailey agreed to part of that argument, ruling that "the evidence introduced touching on the unknown and unnamed bodies from the Insane Hospital should be withdrawn."[356] When the members of the jury entered the courtroom, Bailey instructed them not to consider such evidence.

The courtroom crowd grew restless as morning dragged on, so much so that Judge Bailey had to "rap his gavel in an attempt to secure order."[357] The judge "appeared to be utterly worn out by the constant grind of the proceedings."[358] The case surely took an emotional toll from all participants, especially when the trial spilled out of the courthouse. A yellow Chicago newspaper had printed a fake story claiming that Judge Bailey was threatened with having his house blown up by dynamite. In the concluding days of the trial, such "fake stories in the paper have been rife," according to the *News*.[359] Under threat of lawsuit, the Chicago newspaper retracted it a few days later.[360]

After the courtroom had quieted down, Ruckelshaus began his closing statement:

> *Do not let us be swayed for Dr. Alexander on the one hand nor by public censure on the other. Let us decide his fate according to the law and the evidence…we have reached the stage where poor people have the right to rise up and demand that the same justice be meted out to the rich and influential as is meted out to the poor…here is a man who has occupied an enviable position in this community. He is backed by the medical profession and other influences. He admitted in his testimony that he was unable to procure bodies in a legitimate manner. Yet, he employs a negro, whom he now claims to be insane to procure the bodies for him…let the father, mother, brother, and sister, who are now at their fireside hoping and praying that their dead will rest in peace, know that you are doing your duty. Say to the gang of graverobbers that they must suffer for the grief, anxiety and sorrow they have caused others. Bring this matter home to yourself. Your wife in a pickling vat.* [361]

The defense gave its closing statements after lunch. As they had throughout the trial, Alexander's lawyers appealed to the jury's racism. Martin Hugg spoke for about two hours, mostly trashing the Black ghouls, although he managed also to compare Alexander to the saviors of the Republic:

> *Abraham Lincoln split rails in southern Indiana; General Grant hauled wood into St. Louis, and my client in a humbler way belongs to this class. With no hope ahead of him he struggled in the dark hours and toiled that he might some day take his proper place among his fellowmen. This community has been poisoned against him because he did not have a chance to tell his story before this avalanche of dirt and filth swept down upon him.* [362]

As for Cantrell, Hugg set about to dehumanize him:

> *Would you send a reputable citizen, well known for probity and honesty, to the penitentiary on lying statements of a black, heinous, slimy creature like Cantrell? You can see the devil in this burly black monster's determination to convict this innocent man. This moral monster preached and robbed graves alternatively. He embezzled church funds while preaching the word of God. This shameless hypocrite, wife deserter and thief said on the witness stand that he knew something of the murder of Doc Lung.* [363]

JNO. M. BAILEY

Lawyer. Criminal Law a Specialty

John Marion Bailey, special judge appointed for Alexander's trial. *Library of Congress.*

"Whom will you believe," Hugg rhetorically asked the jury, "this reputable citizen or this pack of beasts?"[364]

The trial was over by the evening of Wednesday, February 12. The next day, Judge Bailey had the stenographer prepare forty-four pages of typewritten notes for the jury. The judge reminded jurors only to consider verdicts on the four counts: taking the body of Rose Neidlinger, knowing that her corpse was obtained illegally; concealing her body; buying her body; and having in his possession a corpse that was obtained without the permission of the family. Alexander faced three to five years, one to three years, one to three years and two to five years in prison, respectively, for each count.[365]

Alexander and his wife were also placed at this time under police protection as the jury deliberated. Some enraged Indianapolitan had threatened the doctor's life. Sheriff Metzger told the *News* that a "young man connected with one of the families that has suffered from the depredations of the graverobbers was heard making threats in the court house corridor. He was talking excitedly and crying, repeating that Dr. Alexander would get a bullet through his head if the jury let him go."[366]

The next day, jury foreman William Gimble informed Judge Bailey "that the jury disagreed, and that it was not possible for them to reach a verdict."[367] Their discussions were so heated during the previous day's deliberations that James White, the cigar salesman, suffered a heart attack.[368] An unmoved Bailey rejected the outcome and told the jury to go back and reach a verdict by Sunday morning.

When Lord's Day rolled around, Gimble told Bailey the same: "We have been unable to reach an agreement and it is my opinion that a verdict from this jury is improbable."[369] Faulkner, Brown, Davis, Eickmann, Gimble, Pasquier and Lingenfelter all voted for acquittal, while Hussey, Lister, Cook and White voted for conviction.

Alexander was a free man, as the case ended in a hung jury. Ruckelshaus made it clear to reporters that he would "call the case of Dr. J.C. Alexander for a rehearing some time after the adjournment of the present grand jury and when all indictments returned by it have been disposed of."[370]

The trial made national press and embarrassed Hoosier politicians. In an attempt to "fix" the graverobbing problem, the Indiana General Assembly passed a "bill for an act for the promotion of anatomical science and to prevent the desecration of graves."[371] The new law attempted to create a legal way for medical colleges to easily obtain cadavers. Too little, too late.

CHAPTER 10

INTERMISSION

antrell and his fellow ghouls were just one of several graverobbing rings resurrecting in central Indiana. However, as African Americans in a bigoted city, they received a disproportionate amount of public attention and harsher legal repercussions than their white counterparts.

This wasn't true in Hamilton County, where angry citizens sought justice against white body snatchers who had operated with impunity for years. In early March 1903, Cantrell was summoned to testify in front of a Hamilton County grand jury to discuss what he knew about Hampton West.[372] On March 6, Cantrell, accompanied by Cass Connaway and IPD detectives Asch and Manning, arrived in Noblesville to make a "full confession of his relations with men of this county, who, he says, have been robbing graves in nearly every cemetery in the county for seven or eight years."[373]

West was still being held in jail on charges for stealing the bodies of Walter Manship and Newton Bracken from Beaver Cemetery just east of Fishers.[374] Even though West had begged Cantrell two months prior to not disclose incriminating details, Rufus apparently told Hamilton County grand jurors what he knew about West's end of the operation. The newspaper reports from this date aren't clear as to what all he divulged, but Connaway later told a reporter that Cantrell had given testimony "to implicate ten or twelve people in this county, some of whom are residents of Noblesville and prominently connected" in the trafficking of dead bodies.[375]

The grand jury determined that Hamp West and his lieutenants were responsible for all graverobbing in southern Hamilton County. The jury also learned that the body snatchers were territorial. West often clashed with

Dedication of the Soldiers and Sailors Monument, May 15, 1902. *From* The Journal Handbook of Indianapolis, *Indianapolis–Marion County Public Library.*

Cantrell over turf disputes in cemeteries along the Marion-Hamilton county border. At some point, the two ghouls worked out an agreement to only rob graves in their respective counties. Cantrell also served as a bagman for the Hamilton County graverobbers, receiving a small fee from West to deliver cadavers, as all the medical schools were in Indy. The "local people would steal the bodies and secret them to a designated place, and Cantrell would take them to the Indianapolis colleges."[376] Some corpses were even floated down the White River to Broad Ripple "in boats and hauled to the colleges in wagons."[377] After Cantrell finished his grand jury interview, he took a tour of downtown Noblesville, under guard of course, and "offered photographs of himself for sale."[378]

A few days later, Cantrell, along with Sam Martin and Walter Daniels, were again called by the grand jury in Noblesville. Together with Adolph Asch and Chauncey Manning, the ghouls arrived to answer new questions. The *News* reported that "it is understood that some prominent citizens of Hamilton county will be charged by the grand jury with being implicated in the robbery of graves. It is believed that the grand jury will return seven or eight indictments."[379]

Left: Hampton West's mugshot photo from 1903. *Indiana State Archives*.

Below: The White River at Broad Ripple. Hamilton County ghouls floated corpses down the river to Broad Ripple. *From* The Journal Handbook of Indianapolis, *Indianapolis–Marion County Public Library.*

Cantrell and Martin also recounted a tale to grand jurors about a gun battle that had supposedly taken place between Cantrell and West "over the possession of a corpse."[380] Apparently, Stout and West surprised Rufus and his ghouls as they were digging into a grave one evening. Stout drew his gun and began firing. Rufus shot back, which led to a small skirmish.

During the gunfight, according to Cantrell, Stout shot and killed William Gray, one of Rufus's fellow graverobbers. If you'll recall, this was the "Billy Gray" whom Cantrell had asked William Coffelt about back in January. It was later rumored that Gray escaped to West Virginia after the fight, but Cantrell was "of the opinion that Gray had been killed and his body disposed of by West and Stout."[381]

Stout, who was also testifying to the Hamilton County grand jury on the same day, denied the allegation. Cantrell had told the grand jurors that he shot Stout in the arm during the gunfight. When the jury asked about this, Stout emphatically denied it, even offering "to strip and show the jury that he had never been shot, but was told that it was not necessary."[382]

The grand jury didn't find the accusation of Billy Gray's murder credible but did indict Hampton West for stealing the bodies of Newton Bracken and Walter Manship from Beaver Cemetery. Lucius Stout was indicted for stealing the body of Walter Manship. The judge set bail for both men at $1,500. Stout could afford his and awaited trial at home, but West, who was already in jail, could not.

Cantrell was also subpoenaed in early March to testify in front of a Cook County grand jury in Chicago. The salacious and mostly false news reports in that city had caused a stir among Chicagoans. Cook County investigators had questions about their own graverobbing problem and believed that Cantrell had answers.[383] When Judge Alford learned of the subpoena, he issued a court order preventing Cantrell from leaving the state: "I will not allow Cantrell to get beyond the jurisdiction of this court. He can go anywhere in Indiana under the care of a guard, but he cannot leave the state. He is wanted here and must stay here."[384]

In the middle of the month, another Indianapolis grand jury returned new indictments against Cantrell and Joseph Alexander, "charging them with conspiring in the theft and disposition of the body of Rose Neidlinger."[385] Dr. Alexander was again arrested, although he made his $1,000 bail. Cantrell could not afford his and remained behind bars. Prosecutor Ruckelshaus requested that the court schedule a new trial in April.

After Alexander's re-arrest, the mysterious and likely fictitious Wallace Simms relaunched his letter writing campaign. In addition to sending the usual missives to Indy newspapers and police officers, Simms wrote to the Chinese ambassador in Washington D.C., Liang Cheng,[386] "asserting that the murderers [of Doc Lung] were negroes who are also implicated in the grave-robbing cases, and that they can be apprehended if the officials do their duty."[387]

Lung's case remained unsolved since Doc Gung Thee's exoneration the year before. The Simms letter sparked renewed interest. Ambassador Cheng sent a letter to the U.S. Secretary of State John Hay requesting intervention in the matter. Hay sent the petition to Indiana's governor, Winfield Durbin, who then dispatched it to the Marion County prosecutor John Ruckelshaus. In Simms's original letter to the ambassador, he indicated that several African American men had broken into Doc Lung's laundry to rob him, but when Lung arrived unexpectedly, he was stabbed by the robbers, who then fled into the night. Simms also suggested that Cantrell was in on the robbery, perhaps even participating by providing "knock out drops" to make the theft easier.[388]

Just as they had before, the city's detectives did not find Simms or his letters credible. With the exception of a barber named Lewis Brown, who told reporters that he was a personal acquaintance of Simms, no one else knew or had ever heard of the mysterious letter writer. Cantrell still believed that the author was Dr. Frank Wright, telling the *Journal* "that many of the charges made in the Simms letters were known to only Cantrell and the doctor."[389] The *Indianapolis News* concurred, writing that the affair might be a "deep-laid plot on the part of friends of Dr. Alexander to increase the prejudice against the negroes, and thus weaken their testimony at the coming trial of Dr. Alexander."[390] Frank Wright, big surprise, denied being Simms but did state that Cantrell had tried to sell Lung's body to his medical college.

The whole Simms character seems kind of ridiculous, but that doesn't mean that Cantrell wasn't somehow involved with or knew something about Lung's murder. Cantrell had testified during Alexander's trial that all he knew came from Dr. Wright. However, several witnesses stated that Rufus flaunted several bloodstained Chinese coins not long after the killing, hinting that they belonged to the launderer.

Rufus again denied killing Lung but admitted that he had considered stealing his body. In his version of the story, Cantrell was hired by Dr. Wright to retrieve the launderer's corpse. One evening, not long after the murder, Wright phoned Cantrell at the Walhalla Saloon, where the ghoul was working as a porter. The doctor, according to Cantrell, wanted Lung's

The Indianapolis Journal Building in 1902. *From* The Journal Handbook of Indianapolis, *Indianapolis–Marion County Public Library.*

body because his ethnicity would be of interest to his students. Wright told the resurrectionist that "you fellows can get anything you go after. I want the body, as it is worth a good deal as a curiosity in a dissecting room."[391]

Cantrell replied, "I told Dr. Wright I had a good job and did not intend to do any more work for the colleges for poor pay."[392] Wright countered that "he would give double price for the body of the Chinese, and I quit my job as porter, intending to go after it."[393] Cantrell failed in his task after learning that Lung was buried in closely watched and guarded Crown Hill Cemetery.

The police didn't believe that Cantrell was involved, "confident that neither Martin nor Cantrell had anything to do with the murder, although they believed Cantrell, at least, knows all about the murder and the identity of the murderer."[394] Detectives also questioned the validity of Wright's claim, asking why Dr. Wright didn't immediately report to police when Cantrell offered to sell him Lung's body.

All evidence was turned over to a Marion County grand jury. Those empaneled reviewed it and again questioned Cantrell and Martin. Dr. Wright was also called to testify, but he ignored the request. Cantrell denied killing Lung but did tell grand jurors another interesting anecdote about Wright. Two years prior, a body was found in the sluiceway near the Riverside Park Dam. The man "who died at the Lighthouse Mission, and who was buried in the poor farm cemetery"[395] was taken to Dr. Wright, who "dissected the body and turned it over to [Cantrell] to dispose of. Cantrell said he tied it in a sack with weights and threw it in the river."[396] Cantrell told the jury that the body was that of Samuel Moore, but a newspaper article at the time indicated that it was William Greatheart.[397]

The jury also interviewed Cassius Willis, the undertaker who Rufus accused of involvement in the body snatching ring back in October. Willis told the jury that he ran into Cantrell soon after Lung's murder, boasting that he knew something about it, but he did not implicate himself.[398]

Alexander's attorney, John Spahr, was also subpoenaed to testify. Spahr initially refused, citing attorney-client privilege, but later changed his mind. Spahr told the grand jurors that he had information from Buford Cowley,

JNO. O. SPAHR
Lawyer

John Spahr, Alexander's lawyer. *Library of Congress.*

118

one of the imprisoned ghouls at the Marion County Jail. Supposedly, Cowley had overheard Cantrell boasting to Sam Martin about committing the murder.

The grand jury submitted its recommendations to Judge Alford and Prosecutor Ruckelshaus. On March 24, police detectives interviewed Cantrell extensively behind closed doors about what he knew regarding Lung's murder. Later in the week, Ollie Sanders, Nimbus Davidson and James Andrews were arrested and charged for the murder of Doc Lung. A fourth accomplice, Jesse Baker, had also been in on the killing but was himself murdered by Herman Wright in a saloon brawl some months later. Sanders confessed to the whole thing—a robbery gone wrong. All arrestees were Black, but none of them was a resurrectionist.[399] Later in the year, Davidson was found guilty of manslaughter and sentenced to two to fourteen years, while Andrews was given life imprisonment. Sanders turned state's evidence and later was released on his own recognizance. The police denied that Cantrell had provided any evidence or information that led to the murderers' arrest. However, the *News* did note that Cantrell had a great "dinner from a down-town restaurant" not long after.[400]

Just to be sure, police detectives opened Lung's grave. The body of the murdered launderer was found safe in his tomb at Crown Hill Cemetery.[401] Lung had been sealed in a steel casket because members of the Chinese community in Indianapolis "were afraid the body would be stolen."[402]

Chapter 11
Sam Martin's Trial

Rufus Cantrell began April 1903 with a hearing to determine his soundness of mind. The proceeding was granted after his brother Nelson filed an "affidavit of insanity against Cantrell" with Emerichsville's justice of the peace, Jacob Emerich.[403] As the law required, Justice Emerich held a commission hearing to determine the matter. Emerich served as chair with Drs. Frank Wynne and Ernest Reyer as commissioners. You'll recall that Reyer was the physician who called Cantrell a moral imbecile during Alexander's trial.

The affidavit was prepared by Cantrell's new lawyers, Taylor Groninger and Frank McCray. The newspaper reports suggest that Cantrell recently hired the two as additional attorneys or perhaps as a replacement for Cass Connaway, although the reasons were unclear.

There's a deeper story here that I can't figure out. If you recall from the first chapter, Groninger was the lawyer who, on behalf of his client, the pawnbroker Emil Mantell, tipped off police about Cantrell's suspicious activity when purchasing guns. Groninger told Mantell that he "was familiar with the name of Rufus Cantrell, and knew his reputation as a ghoul." In other words, the man who helped turn Cantrell into police was now his lawyer? Fishy.

Connaway, who had been Cantrell's attorney since the fall, apparently "was not consulted before the action was taken, and last night, expressed his indignation at the procedure, and said he knew nothing of it." In fact, Rufus didn't even know of it.

Sam Martin's mugshot photos from 1903. *Indiana State Archives.*

In order to obtain an insanity hearing, an affidavit attesting to one's mental instability had to be filed with a judge or justice of the peace, which prompted a commission. The *News* reported that the "inquest was peddled about the county until a justice of the peace was found to handle the case."[404] Justice Emerich "did not know who filed the papers, or anything about the case, except that Nelson Cantrell, a brother of Rufus, came before him with a constable and made the affidavit."[405]

All hell broke loose at the hearing on April 10. When the commission opened, Marion County prosecutors immediately interrupted the first witness call and "accused McCray and Groninger of influencing the negro ghouls in the jail not to appear as witnesses against Dr. Alexander" and for Cantrell to escape prison at a mental health institution.[406] The court had scheduled Dr. Alexander's new trial for the following week. How convenient it would be if Cantrell was determined to be insane, thus damaging his credibility as the state's star witness. Plus, if the strategy served to help Cantrell escape a state penitentiary at a mental health hospital, all the better.

At the hearing, Ruckelshaus told Justice Emerich, "McCray is only trying to make a grandstand play here. We intend to try Dr. Alexander next Monday. I want to tell this commission that attorneys McCray and Groninger have talked with Sam Martin, Sol Grady, William Jones and

Walter Daniels, and they have influenced these negroes not to testify against Dr. Alexander."[407] As for Rufus, Ruckelshaus argued that "the trial of Dr. Alexander depended on Cantrell's testimony. To declare the witness an insane man would be to allow an indicted man to escape trial."

McCray bluntly interrupted, arguing that Marion County prosecutors had no jurisdiction at a county insanity hearing. The attorneys descended into a shouting match, with Ruckelshaus accusing McCray of "laying a 'deadfall' for the negroes to fall in."

McCray shot back, "It was not incumbent upon the commission to notify the prosecutor that an inquest was to be held. The State of Indiana is not a party."

Justice Emerich concluded that Ruckelshaus, or any party, could have the necessary time to prepare witnesses and was entitled to a continuance, if so requested. Prosecutors immediately moved for one, which Emerich granted.

'SQUIRE EMERICH.

Justice of the Peace Jacob Emrich, from the *Indianapolis News*, April 10, 1903. *Hoosier State Chronicles*.

At the bang of the gavel, Cass Connaway rushed into the courtroom and began yelling at Groninger, questioning his motives and accusing him of working for the city's medical establishment.

Groninger shouted back, "I don't want you or any other man to impugn my motives."

"I know what your motives are and I can prove every word I say," Connaway snapped back. "You are not trying to assist [Cantrell] and you know it! You are conspiring to down him for the benefit of Dr. Alexander! I just this moment came from the jail, and I know what you are up to."[408] Both men had to be restrained by colleagues.

Connaway later admitted to a reporter that Groninger had asked to help defend Cantrell, a request to which the lawyer agreed, apparently without much thought or oversight. He had no idea how McCray came to the defense. Cantrell didn't even know that an affidavit describing his insanity had been filed. A reporter asked him, "Did you authorize your attorneys to bring the proceeding?"

"I did not," replied Cantrell.

"Did you want to go to the insane asylum instead of the penitentiary?"

"I don't see what good it will do to send me to the asylum. No, I don't want to go, but I do want to get out of jail."[409]

Later that day, Connaway confronted Rufus at the Marion County Jail, demanding that he pick a lawyer. After the conversation, Connaway stormed "out in a huff." Cantrell told reporters that he "guessed he had lost his best friend."[410]

Alexander's attorneys denied being involved in any way. Martin Hugg told the *Journal* that "our theory of defense is on the innocence of Dr. Alexander and not on the insanity of Rufus Cantrell…you can be assured that Dr. Alexander's attorneys have not resorted to any trick to clear their client."[411]

Judge Alford was furious and ordered Cantrell confined at a hearing. "There has been too much horseplay in this case and I had a notion to say so in my order," thundered Alford. "These men will certainly be tried," insane or not. He just needed a special judge, "a man who has the courage to sit on this bench and try them."[412] Alford continued his fire and brimstone, setting trial dates for the imprisoned resurrectionists: Martin on April 15, Cantrell on April 20, Donnell on April 24, Grady on April 27, Jones on April 30 and Daniels on May 4.

As expected, Sam Martin, Sol Grady, William Jones and Isom Donnell all refused to testify for prosecutors at Alexander's new trial. The ever nimble Cantrell, however, let it be known that he was still on the fence. All five knew that they were "getting the worst end of the deal, and that they will gain nothing by testifying."[413]

Charles Brown in 1897, special judge during Cantrell's trial. *Library of Congress.*

On the following Monday morning, as Alexander's trial began, Ruckelshaus moved for an indefinite continuance, as he had no witnesses to support his case. Alford granted the motion after hearing no protest from the defense. Alexander once again escaped consequences for his crimes.

As for the other resurrectionists still languishing in the Marion County Jail, "we now propose to go ahead with the trials of the negroes," said Ruckelshaus. "There will be no more delays."[414] Judge Alford received an answer to his request for "courageous" special judges. William Thornton was to hear Sam Martin's case, and Charles F. Coffin would hear Cantrell's.[415] Yes, you read that right, a man with the surname Coffin was to judge a graverobbing trial.[416]

In addition to Cantrell and his compatriots, McCray and Groninger also had become the attorneys for Ollie Sanders. Cantrell, as you'll remember, likely provided information to police implicating Sanders and two others in Doc Lung's killing.[417] Groninger would go on to secure a deal for Sanders as his lawyer: freedom in exchange for state testimony.

Sam Martin's trial began two days later on Wednesday, April 15, 1903. McCray and Groninger served as Martin's lawyers, with Ruckelshaus prosecuting the case. The *News* reported that attorneys quickly ran through a pool of ninety-two possible jurors, a venire largely and unusually "composed of prominent business men."[418] Most potential jurors were dismissed on account that "nearly every man drawn said he had read the accounts of the grave robberies, and had formed an opinion of the guilt of the negroes charged with the crimes, and that he did not believe his opinion could be changed by the evidence."[419]

During the selection, McCray asked Alexander Mueller, a saloon keeper, if he could be a fair juror: "You are sure you could deal fairly with this man?"

"Yes," replied Mueller.

"Have you ever declared yourself on the question?"

"No."

McCray shot back, "Did you not, a few minutes ago, say to a man in this room that they ought to take the whole gang of ghouls out and lynch them and save the county the expense?"[420] A disgusted McCray dismissed Mueller.

Out of options, the bailiff just grabbed people off the street and even "invaded the county treasurer's office and summoned a number of taxpayers lined up before the window."[421] The effort worked, and by the afternoon, both sides had agreed on twelve men to sit as Martin's jurors: Samuel Grube, Theodore Marcy, L.N. Cotton, George Stradling, C.C. Thompson, Zimri C. Lewis, John D. Hayworth, Thomas Hessong, Frank Fessler, William Thorne, Lewis Meyers and John Millhouse.[422]

McCray tried to have the case thrown out on the grounds that the recent anatomy law passed by the General Assembly had technically repealed the 1879 law under which Martin was accused. They also moved to dismiss Martin's confession to detectives, claiming that it was made under duress. The *News* questioned these tactics, citing that Martin had "pleaded not guilty to the charge, but at no time have his attorneys declared in court that he did not commit the crimes he is charged with."

The state sought to prove Martin's guilt by using his own testimony against him. Prosecutors first called to the stand A.C. Metcalf, the stenographer during Martin's grand jury interview. Metcalf read the testimony, where

Sam Martin's mugshot photo from 1903. *Indiana State Archives.*

the graverobber admitted the "complicity in robbing the graves of Wallace Johnson, Glendora Gates, Catherine Doehring, John Sargent, Mrs. Perry Shaw and Johanna Stilz."[423]

Walter Carpenter, the stenographer at Alexander's trial, testified next. He read Martin's testimony, where the ghoul admitted that "he had been in the graverobbing business about four years, and had disposed of about $90 worth of bodies to the Central College and had received the money from Dr. Alexander."[424]

The state rested after hearing testimony from George and Daniel Stilz, Manson Neidlinger and Frank Doehring. After a short recess, McCray opened for the defense, in which he argued that all the ghouls' testimony had been taken under duress. McCray also accused the police of plying the resurrectionists with alcohol and that Connaway tried to railroad Martin, Cantrell and the rest of the African American ghouls into guilty pleas. McCray said that "he would show that Connaway was in touch with detectives Asch and Manning in regard to the cases and they had on one occasion got the prisoners drunk." Connaway, according to the defense, "plied them with whisky, and besides favoring them in many other ways, assured them of immunity from punishment if they would assist the police."[425] McCray concluded saying that Martin "finally yielded to the importunities, solicitations and threats."[426]

McCray first called to the stand Garfield Buckner, Martin's fellow resurrectionist. Buckner refused to testify and stared ahead "owl like" after each question. Buckner was held in contempt, fined five dollars and sentenced to thirty days in jail.

Cantrell testified next. The body snatcher said that the ghouls' confessions were secured "because threats and promises of leniency had been made."[427] Cantrell had hired Connaway on a recommendation from James Collins, deputy prosecutor. Cantrell told the jury that "Connaway had told Martin and him that if they would confess and engage him as their attorney he would see that they got off easily."[428] Cantrell also said that Connaway once claimed to have supported Ruckelshaus and Benedict during their elections, so much so that he "could call on them for favors."[429]

Connaway, according to Cantrell, had provided alcohol and "liberally plied him during the wait in the grand jury anteroom."[430] He told the resurrectionists that if they would all implicate "the other prominent physicians identified with the Indiana College so much fuss would be raised and so much money brought into the case that none of us would ever be convicted."[431]

The defense concluded its case with testimony from fellow ghoul Sol Grady. He told the jury "about a conversation he had overheard between detectives Asch and Manning relative to the favors being show Cantrell and the possibility of release if all the negro prisoners would help the State in the prosecution of Dr. Alexander and the other accused physicians."[432]

The state followed by calling rebuttal witnesses, including Deputy Sheriff John Comer, who emphatically denied that whisky ever

Sol Grady's mugshot photo from 1903. *Indiana State Archives.*

entered his jail. Detectives Asch and Manning testified to the same. Deputy prosecutor Collins told jurors that he had indeed recommended Connaway after the ghouls got nowhere with their first attorney, W.E. Henderson. Collins told Cantrell "that Connaway was a lawyer of good reputation and of much promise…he could get no better man in Indianapolis to work hard for him."[433]

The October grand jury foreman, Charles Kahl, testified that he never saw the ghouls intoxicated during testimony. Judge George Stubbs testified that no one was ever drunk or drinking during his proceedings.

The next morning, Connaway was called as the state's last rebuttal witness. The attorney "denied emphatically that he had supplied the negroes with liquor or had endeavored to secure confessions from them while they were under the influence of liquor."[434]

McCray and Groninger argued in their closing statements that Martin had made his confession "against the defendant's will, and under duress, and for that reason it shouldn't be held against him."[435] Groninger concluded that Martin was a "poor defenseless man, without a dollar" and that the new body snatching law made the 1879 legislation moot. Ruckelshaus countered in his closing statement by saying that "if Martin is without a dollar, I wonder if there is any truth to the rumor that the attorneys for the negroes are being retained by the doctors" and that there was "no coercion in obtaining the confession from Martin, who was clearly guilty in the eye of the law."[436]

The 1876 Marion County Courthouse as it looked in 1902. *From* The Journal Handbook of Indianapolis, *Indianapolis–Marion County Public Library.*

McCray openly challenged the point about being paid for by the doctors, but Judge Thornton stopped the fracas and fined both lawyers five dollars. He reminded the jury that "a confession of a defendant made under inducement is not sufficient to warrant a conviction without corroborating testimony" and that "for the purpose of the trial of this case the act of 1879 is still in force."[437] With that, the jury was excused to deliberate.

The jury reached a verdict within twenty-five minutes, finding Sam Martin guilty as charged. Judge Thornton sentenced him to three to ten years in state prison. After hearing the outcome, Isom Donnell and Walter Daniels fired Groninger and McCray.

CHAPTER 12

THE KING'S TRIAL

What, exactly, were McCray and Groninger up to? Were they indeed being paid by the doctors? If so, whose interests were they really serving? Why did the ghouls change lawyers just before their trials?

Cantrell's trial began on Monday, April 20, 1903, with Special Judge Charles Coffin presiding. As proceedings began, McCray made a motion to dismiss, deploying the same strategy he used during Martin's trial. McCray argued that the new 1903 anatomy law repealed the old 1879 legislation under which the ghoul was indicted. Coffin overruled the motion, and "a special plea of insanity was filed by the defense and a plea of not guilty entered."[438]

The defense then made a bold but just second motion. McCray "sprang a small sensation by moving that one-half of the jury be made up of colored men of Marion county, eligible to act as jurors."[439] Regardless of who was paying his fees, McCray rightly asserted that Cantrell wasn't going to get a fair trial with an all-white Marion County jury. When Judge Coffin "recovered his breath he overruled the motion."[440] The court then set about selecting twelve white men to serve as Cantrell's peers.[441]

As with Martin's case, both sides had a hard time selecting jurors. Given all of the hullabaloo around the graverobbers in the local, state and national press, finding someone without an opinion proved to be an arduous task. The *News* reported that "every man examined had read of the ghoul cases and most of them had made an expressed opinion."[442]

Rufus Cantrell's mugshot photos from 1903. *Indiana State Archives.*

The attorneys interviewed a venire of eighty-seven potential jurors and by 4:00 p.m. had decided on the following twelve white men: Julius Pennell, H.C. Jackson, Thomas Carson, Christian Resener, John Clough, Charles Reynolds, Peter Pursell, John Wampner, C.H. Waterman, Francis Montgomery, Charles Willette and Robert Nixon.[443] Nixon was later rumored to have paid Dr. Frank Wright's bond the previous fall, although apparently prosecutors didn't believe it.

Cantrell was indicted on four counts: "one count charges him with conspiracy to commit a felony; another with taking the body of Mrs. Rose Neidlinger from the grave; another with concealing the body; and a fourth with having the body in his possession, in connection with Dr. Alexander, for the purpose of dissecting it." The state dropped two of the counts: conspiring to commit a felony and taking Neidlinger's body from the grave. Prosecutors planned to use the same strategy to convict Cantrell as they did with Martin by using the ghoul's own confession and testimony against him. Defense lawyers sought to convince the jury that their client was insane.

The trial ran late that Monday. After deputy prosecutor Charles Benedict made his opening statement, the state again called Walter Carpenter, the stenographer during Alexander's trial. Carpenter re-read Cantrell's testimony, where he admitted to extensive graverobbing in the summer of 1902.

Marion County Courthouse in 1904. *Library of Congress.*

The next morning, the state moved to have Cantrell's discharge papers from the War Department withheld from evidence. The defense had intended to submit it to underscore Cantrell's supposed poor mental health.[444]

The two sides argued the admissibility of such evidence. Ruckelshaus told the judge that if such a document was submitted, the state "will introduce the testimony of witnesses to whom Cantrell is said to have explained the ruses he resorted to in order to obtain his discharge. One of these tricks was to chew soap to make it appear that he was frothing at the mouth."[445] Judge Coffin barred the document from evidence.

The state called Arthur McKee, the assistant at Habich's gun store. McKee testified that he rented guns often to Cantrell and Dr. Alexander. During their exchanges, Cantrell bragged about his graverobbing exploits, telling the clerk that he routinely stole jewelry off the bodies and that he "was King of the Grave Robbers."[446]

Ruckelshaus followed with a series of witnesses to further corroborate Carpenter's reading of Cantrell's testimony. Douglas Case, the proprietor of the Hotel de Hoss livery barn, testified "that he had seen Dr. Alexander and Cantrell at the stable several times."[447] Several other de Hoss employees concurred. W.R. Beard had sold Cantrell a five-dollar ring on loan, with a guarantee from Alexander; a pawnbroker named Charles Medias testified that Rufus had rented guns from him several times; and Joseph Staley, a furniture repairer, told the jury that the ghoul had rented his brace and bit.

Their testimony was followed by that of the victims. Julia Middleton tearfully gave a tragic recounting of finding her daughter's body at Central College, "I told them it was my daughter and I had come for her. They gave her to me and we put her back in the ground." Wesley Gates, Frank Doehring, Manson Neidlinger and Edward Stilz testified in a similar fashion. The state rested after Stilz was dismissed.

Groninger followed with the defense's opening statement, a sweeping description of Cantrell's supposed insanity:

> *While Cantrell lived in Gallatin, Tennessee from the age of one to fifteen years, he suffered from epilepsy; that when twelve years old he was thrown from a horse and his head was injured; that when he was ten or twelve years old he had a delusion that he was called by God to preach, and told his friends that he had talked with God face to face; that while at work in the field he would kneel at the plow and pray and preach from a Biblical text; that he still suffers from delusions and in the jail has preached to prisoners; that when taunted by his friends in Tennessee over his inability to preach he would become profane and once assaulted a minister with his tongue when he refused to ordain him; that he has a violent temper and has attempted the lives of himself and others; that he delighted to call himself "King of the Bryan campaign." and has cards printed with the words, "Rufus Cantrell—the Democratic hero"; that he suffered a sunstroke in Indianapolis, which incapacitated him for work in hot places.*[448]

To nail the point home, Groninger also added that his client had syphilis.[449]

The defense called Cantrell's mother, Sarah, to the stand as their first witness.[450] Sarah testified that her son had a grandfather and an aunt with mental health illness and that Cantrell was prone to fits and spasms. She told the jury that when Rufus was "a boy he had tried to preach and said he had talked with God. Sometimes he would have mad spells and become very violent and profane."[451] Sarah was dismissed and court adjourned.

The next morning, Groninger and McCray called several doctors to testify about Cantrell's mental health. Dr. W.B. Fletcher said that Rufus was a "moral degenerate."[452] Dr. Wynne told the jury that someone matching

Courtroom sketch of Cantrell's trial, from the *Indianapolis News*, April 20, 1903. *Hoosier State Chronicles.*

Cantrell's actions would be of "unsound mind, but not wholly irresponsible. Cantrell might have impulses over which he had no control."[453] Dr. Ernest Reyer testified to the effects of sunstroke.

The defense concluded by calling John Kimble, the county jailer. Kimble testified that he saw "Cantrell crying several times, and heard him preach in jail."[454] When Kimble was dismissed, the defense rested.

The state followed with a series of rebuttal witnesses, who declared Cantrell to be quite sane, including Talbott Moore, October's grand jury foreman; Horace Woods, a livery barn attendant; and William Craig, a veterinarian. John Comer, the former deputy sheriff, testified that he recently told the ghoul, "Rufus, they are trying to make you crazy."

"Yes," replied Cantrell, "that's to their interest, but I am no more crazy than Spaan or Hugg."

The state then called a series of reporters to the stand, all of whom had interviewed Cantrell, including Frank Baker, N.C. Wright, Ray Thompson and Kent Cooper. All four found Rufus to be of sound mind. So did Martin Hyland, an IPD captain, and Detective Adolph Asch. Charles L. Bieler, the secretary at Anderson Foundry where Cantrell once worked, thought the ghoul was "very much sane."[455]

On Thursday, the lawyers concluded with their closing statements, after which the jury broke to deliberate Cantrell's guilt or innocence. The jury had reached a decision by 8:30 p.m., finding Cantrell guilty. The verdict was delivered by Robert Nixon, the jury foreman: "We, the jury, find the defendant, Rufus Cantrell, guilty of the first and fourth counts of indictment as charged, theft and conspiracy in the theft of the body of Rose Niedlinger."[456]

Whether Nixon knew the doctors or not was unclear, as the newspapers never really concluded one way or another, but they did print the rumor. In the jury's first round, eleven found Cantrell sane and voted guilty, but Nixon disagreed and voted to acquit on account of the ghoul's insanity. However, three votes later, all twelve were in agreement: Cantrell was sane and guilty of both charges.

Rufus seemed to take the news with stoicism as he "preserved the same stolid demeanor which he has exhibited during his trial."[457] The *News* reported that "Cantrell was in an apparently happy frame of mind when he appeared in court to-day."[458] After the verdict was read, Judge Coffin sentenced him to three to ten years for the first count and two to fourteen years on the second, to be served concurrently at Indiana's Jeffersonville Penitentiary. When court adjourned, Cantrell thanked his lawyers and

CHARLES FRANKLIN COFFIN.

FREMONT ALFORD
Judge Criminal Court Marion County

Left: Charles Coffin, special judge appointed for Cantrell's trial. *Library of Congress*.

Right: Fremont Alford, Indianapolis Criminal Court judge. *Library of Congress*.

told deputy prosecutor Benedict that "he bore him no ill will."[459] The resurrectionist was then taken back to jail.

The fallout from the trial set the agenda for how the rest would go. Prosecutors first sought plea deals with the remaining resurrectionists to "save the county additional expense."[460] The body snatchers declined and pleaded not guilty at trial hearings.[461] Ruckelshaus seemed to have lost interest at this point. He told a reporter, "I do not believe that Dr. Joseph Alexander will ever be brought to trial again to answer the charge of graverobbing."[462] Because the witnesses claimed to be coerced and possibly insane, "I doubt if a jury could be secured that would convict the doctor on evidence given to them."[463]

Cantrell said he had additional information to give to grand jurors and wasn't immediately taken to Jeffersonville, but this was more or less a ruse to stay in Indianapolis to meet with his family before heading south. When Judge Alford learned of this, "he ordered the sheriff to take Cantrell away to-day."[464]

The rural residents of Hamilton County were irate at the outcome. Their rage wasn't aimed at Cantrell but at Dr. Alexander, Hampton West and Judge Bailey. When it became clear that many of the ghouls would evade justice, several farmers at Fishers Station burned the resurrectionists in effigy. On April 23:

> [A]*n indication of the bitter feeling against the graverobbers in the farming districts north of the city, along the Hamilton county line, and the strong sentiment against the action of the Marion county court in failing to convict Dr. J.C. Alexander, was shown last night, when a crowd of indignant men burned in effigy Dr. Alexander; Hampton West, of Hamilton County, charged with graverobbing, and attorney John M. Bailey, who acted as special judge.*[465]

The rioters even erected scaffolding to hang the straw figures along Main Street, but a local railroad agent convinced them to burn the dummies on the ground. The effigies were cut down and torched in the middle of the road as farmers shouted, "Death to the graverobbers."[466] On top of the unused scaffolding, the people of Fishers Station had crudely painted an extrajudicial warning: "Justice to Bailey, Alexander and West."[467]

Chapter 13

The Confederates' Trial

Ruckelshaus moved to try the remaining cases in May 1903, although only a few ever made it to court. The newspaper reports suggest that prosecutors were exhausted and ready to move on. On May 7, Isom Donnell, on advice from his new attorney, "pleaded guilty to-day to the second count in the indictment against him and received from one to three years in the State's prison at Michigan City."[468] Prosecutors had charged Donnell with taking and concealing the body of Glendora Gates. During the sentencing, the judge told him that, unfortunately, he wouldn't be housed with his cousin Rufus in prison. This sat fine with Isom, who told the judge, "I've seen too much of Cantrell already."[469] Two days later, Sol Grady and William Jones pleaded the same and were sentenced to one to three years at Michigan City.[470]

Prosecutors made another halfhearted attempt to bring Joseph Alexander to trial, but nothing ever came from their inquiries.[471] The *News* speculated that it was the "belief of those intimately acquainted with the ghoul cases that Cantrell and his confederates were paid for refusing to testify in a second trial against Dr. Alexander, and that they were led to believe that they might be acquitted if they did not further commit themselves."[472] In late April, the *Journal* reported that "the indictments against the doctors who were implicated in the ghouls scandals still stand, and the bonds will continue in the hands of the sheriff until three terms of court have passed."[473] The indictments all ended up expiring without prosecution. With the exception of Alexander's February trial, not a single other anatomist faced a jury for graverobbing.

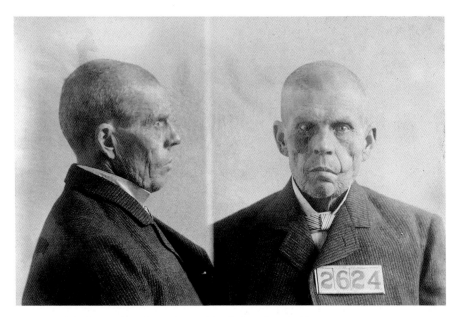

Hampton West's mugshot photos from 1903. *Indiana State Archives.*

Isom Donnell's mugshot photos from 1903. *Indiana State Archives.*

The Marion County Jail in 1902. *From* The Journal Handbook of Indianapolis, *Indianapolis–Marion County Public Library.*

On June 27, Garfield Buckner, Al Hunt, John McEndree, Walter Williams, William McElroy and George Mason were released from prison on their own recognizance. The *Indianapolis Star* told readers that "the charges have not been dismissed against any of them. All but Mason are charged with taking and concealing a corpse. Mason was indicted for disturbing graves. All but McEndree are colored."[474] Prosecutor Ruckelshaus told the *Star*:

> *These men made it possible for us to convict the persons responsible for the grave robbing and they have been fair in the matter from the start. We could probably send some more of them to prison, but they have suffered considerable punishment already and have been straight enough to help convict the real criminals. We feel that they were entitled to more consideration than the leaders.*[475]

Although Marion County's graverobbing cases were winding down that spring, Hamilton County's were just beginning. Lucius Stout of Eagletown, Hamp West's ghoulish lieutenant, was arrested in late March after "a grand jury indictment charged him with helping Hampton West take the body of Walter Manship from its grave in the Beaver cemetery and selling it to a medical college."[476] Stout escaped justice "when it was found that the grand jury indictment charged him with an offense that was committed over two years ago. It is alleged that Manship's grave was robbed in January of 1901."[477] The statute of limitations for the crime had run out, and Stout walked free. With Stout's release, the *News* told readers that "this clears the docket of graverobbery cases."[478]

This wasn't entirely true. There was still the matter of Wade Hampton "Hamp" West, who sat languishing in the Hamilton County Jail under charges that he stole the body of Newton Bracken from the Beaver Creek Cemetery.[479] In June 1903, the *Hamilton County Ledger* reported that West was alone—"it seems that all the friends West ever had and his attorneys have deserted him. So far as known he is not being represented by any one and no effort is being made to have his case set for trial."[480]

Supposedly, Frank Baker, an *Indianapolis News* reporter, obtained a jailhouse confession from West around this time in which the ghoul admitted to killing Billy Gray. The interview turned bad when West realized that Baker was a reporter. West began "abusing him, threatened to do him bodily harm and did finally kick Baker in the face."[481] The reporter quickly deescalated the situation by brandishing a revolver.

The trial of Hampton West got underway in July 1903. The court had pushed it back several times "on account of many of the witnesses who are farmers being busy with the harvest" that summer.[482] Although West had plundered a huge number of southern Hamilton County graves, the ghoul was only on trial for stealing Bracken's body in September 1901, well within the window to prosecute.

The state's lead witnesses were Rufus Cantrell and Sam Martin. Elmer Gorman, a prison guard, brought both ghouls up from Jeffersonville. On the train ride to Indy, Cantrell joked to Gorman that he should "let the people know that Rufus, King of the Grave Robbers, and his fast runner Martin, were in town."[483]

Upon arriving in Indy, Cantrell, true to form, told reporters that he "had in his possession a vast amount of valuable information which could be used to advantage by the detectives in this city, but further than that, refused to talk."[484] Cantrell was given a closed-door interview with Asch and Manning. "What he told detectives is not known. Martin backed Cantrell in all his statements. The detectives took Cantrell to see his wife and mother during the evening."[485]

The newspapers speculated that Cantrell had shared information about the mysterious disappearance of Carrie Selvage. In March 1900, Selvage, "a patient at the Union State Hospital, 1315 Capitol Avenue, north, escaped from the institution, Sunday morning, and all efforts to find her have been in vain. She was dressed in a light blue wrapper and felt slippers when she left the hospital."[486] Selvage was a public school teacher before she experienced a severe mental health crisis and was hospitalized. She supposedly walked out of the Union State Hospital that March and was never seen again. Family members searched for months in vain. The canal was even dredged at one point and her brother Joseph hired a clairvoyant, but Selvage had simply vanished.[487]

According to the *News*, Cantrell told detectives that "Miss Selvage, when she escaped from the Union State Hospital, where she was confined as a patient, fell into the hands of the Hamilton county man, and was imprisoned in a log hut on his farm for several weeks. She was then killed by chloroform and buried in a cemetery about fourteen miles north of Indianapolis. The body was not sent to a college for fear that the authorities would hear of the matter."[488]

Joseph Selvage didn't believe Cantrell at first—at least, he didn't believe the newspaper reports. A day later, Rufus told a reporter that he never told cops such things, saying that the story must have "originated in the brain of some reporter and was intended to turn public opinion against him."[489] The detectives concurred, telling the *Journal* that "Rufus Cantrell never told them one word about the Selvage Case. They said the first intimation they had of the supposed information on that source was read by them in the newspapers."[490]

This reporting was either wrong or made up. Maybe Cantrell and the detectives were lying? Because on July 14, according to the *Journal*, Asch, Manning and Joseph Selvage, accompanied by Cantrell, opened a grave in Union Chapel Cemetery. "A woman's body, badly decomposed, was found, but Mr. Selvage was unable to identify it as that of his sister."[491] Carrie had false teeth, and the woman buried at this grave did not.

The newspaper reports are inconsistent. Did Cantrell actually have information about Selvage? Were the newspapers printing rumors or factual occurrences? As was his custom, Cantrell may also have said different things to different people. On July 15, Rufus promised to divulge everything he knew "if they will only let me alone and promise that I will have the proper treatment if I tell the detectives what I know."[492] The *Journal* noted in the same article that "Cantrell claimed at the jail last night that he had been made a fool of by the detectives, and had been driven around the city merely for the newspaper notoriety of the affair."[493]

Sam Martin had a different theory. He told a reporter that "all the talk which Cantrell was making was a mystery to him. He stated that Cantrell was smoking a peculiar grade of tobacco and was rambling in his speech."[494] Whatever the truth, nothing more happened with the Carrie Selvage case in 1903, but Cantrell's involvement with her disappearance, real or not, was far from over.

Hamp West was represented by an Indianapolis attorney named Newton Harding. He faced off against the Hamilton County prosecutor Fred Hines. West's trial in Noblesville received an enormous amount of public attention and continued to make national headlines. The *Hamilton County Ledger* reported that "the trial is largely attended, the courtroom being almost filled with spectators. Delaware and Fall Creek townships are well represented. The forenoon was taken up with the selection of a jury."[495]

The two sides agreed on twelve Hamilton County farmers as jurors: John Clarke, Fred Creag, William Vaught, N.T. Royer, John Briles, S.D. Stultz, George Jones, Charles Roby, William Stevene, Wesley White, John Foulke and Edward Caslin.[496] West pleaded not guilty.

The state opened, declaring to prove

> that Rufus Cantrell and West were employed by a medical college at Indianapolis to procure bodies for dissecting purposes from Marion and Hamilton counties. By mutual agreement between Cantrell and West it is further alleged that this territory was divided—Cantrell taking Marion county and West Hamilton county. Mr. Hines said that the evidence would show that Cantrell and Samule Martin came to West and the three agreed to rob the grave which Bracken was buried. On the night of the robbery, West was accompanied by a stranger, whose name has not yet appeared in evidence. Bracken was a man who weighed 235 pounds, and it required the strength of all four men to remove the body from the grave.[497]

Hines first called W.F. Bracken to the stand. Newton's brother testified that he discovered the empty grave in May 1902. Martin was called next. He told the jury that he served as the driver on the night in question and noted a white wagon driver, but because the light was minimal, he couldn't say for sure if it was West. Martin concluded that he was under the impression at the time that the Bracken family approved of the resurrection. This was news to Newton's widow, who next testified that she never "had given her consent that the body of her husband might be taken by the medical college."[498]

Cantrell followed the widow on the stand, telling the jury that West once bragged that he "had been robbing graves for seventeen years." The two ghouls met often at night "in Hopewell, Mt. Jackson, Round Hill, Union Chapel, Fairview, White Chapel, Oaklandon, Beaver, and other cemeteries."[499]

As for Albert "Newton" Bracken, the deceased had died in late September 1901 from typhoid fever.[500] Cantrell wanted the body, but because it was in West's territory, the Confederate "consented to let Cantrell come and get the body for $10."[501]

The night of the graverobbery, Cantrell arrived at Beaver Creek Cemetery with John McEndree and another graverobber named Charley Hubbard. At the time of West's trial, Hubbard was serving time in Michigan City for an unrelated murder but was also brought to Noblesville to testify. Cantrell told the jury that the three ghouls met West and Lucius Stout in the cemetery on the evening in question. The Hamilton County ghouls[502] were already digging when Cantrell and his fellow resurrectionists arrived, and "when the body was in the Wagon, Cantrell paid West $10, as per agreement."[503]

Cantrell said that West asked to be paid with two five-dollar bills, so that he could give "half of the money to his companion, known as 'Turtle,' whom Cantrell afterward said was Lucius R. Stout, of Eagletown, the Hamilton County farmer, who lost $3,100 on a fake foot race in Springfield, Illinois last year."[504]

Cantrell also answered questions about his Marion County jailhouse chat with West in November. Hamp had asked Rufus "repeatedly not to implicate him in anything he might say. On one occasion West gave [Cantrell] 50 cents, and promised more money soon."[505] West also reminded Cantrell that if he intended to rat out his fellow resurrectionists, "an oath that had been written in blood would be broken."[506] The state then entered West's January letter to Cantrell into evidence.

The ghoul calmly answered questions under cross-examination. The graverobber "was one of the coolest and most collected witnesses who ever testified in this court. He admitted having preached, was in the undertaking business, tended a truck patch and confessed to being a grave robber but denied that he ever preached at a funeral and stole the body the next night."[507]

Ralph Kane, one of West's attorneys, asked Cantrell several pointed questions about body snatching. In answering one of Kane's questions, Cantrell shot back, "Before my God I say that is not true."

Kane replied, "Don't talk about God. He don't know you."

"That may be true," Cantrell said without missing a beat, "but neither will He know you when this trial is over."[508] The packed Hamilton County Courthouse erupted into laughter as Rufus was dismissed.

Frank Randall, Hamilton County's deputy sheriff, testified next about the authenticity of West's January letter. W.T. Long followed on the stand. A veterinarian from Indy, Long testified that West indeed knew of Cantrell at the time of the former's arrest. Detectives Asch and Manning testified that West had visited Cantrell when the two were briefly held together in the Marion County Jail. The "detectives said that West asked to be allowed to see Cantrell alone. The officers stepped into an adjoining room but did not close the door. They immediately noticed a familiarity between the two and West gave Cantrell something. Later Cantrell said it was fifty cents."[509] The court then adjourned for the weekend.

On the following Monday morning, Ralph Flanders, a farmer who had once lived near West, testified that he "accidentally came across the defendant in a thicket on his farm late one evening, and West was boiling the body of a rather heavy-set man in a large kettle. The head was missing. When Flanders inquired of West where he obtained the corpse, West said that Dr. Joseph Alexander, of Indianapolis, gave it to him."[510]

Then Benjamin Castetter testified seeing West "return from Indianapolis about daylight on the morning after Bracken's body was stolen."[511] Castetter was delivering produce early to Indy when he witnessed West asleep in his wagon along Fall Creek, heading back north to his Hamilton County farm.

The state concluded its case by calling Charley Hubbard to the stand. Hubbard told the jury that he was with Cantrell and West one evening robbing a grave.[512]

Newton Harding gave his opening statement for the defense next. He told the jury that "the evidence would show that the defendant never took any part whatsoever in robbing the grave of Newton Bracken" and that "he was cutting corn on his farm instead of being present at the funeral of Newton Bracken."[513] On the date in which West allegedly had stolen Bracken's body, the ghoul, according to the defense, was at home with his poor sick wife.

Lucius Stout was called first, testifying that he never knew West and wasn't involved in graverobbing. West's son Arthur followed, telling jurors that he slept in the same bed with his father on the night in question. Over the next few days, West family members all claimed on the stand that their father was home with their sick mother the week Bracken's body went missing.

Cantrell was called again, this time by the defense. In an attempt to discredit him, he was asked by defense attorneys about whether detectives had given him beer and whisky in jail. Cantrell denied this, adding that "he could not remember any of the details of his evidence in the Alexander case."[514] How convenient.

After both sides gave their closing statements, the jury began deliberations on the morning of July 16. After eighteen hours, the jury found Hampton West guilty on all counts. The ghoul showed no emotion of any kind when the verdict was read.[515] He was sentenced to three to ten years at Michigan City.

Hampton West's mugshot photo from 1903. *Indiana State Archives.*

West was subdued on his way back to jail. The *Hamilton County Ledger* reported that the "old man told the officer that he did not care so much about the result as one might suppose. He expressed himself as being glad that it was over as he knew now what they intended to do with him."[516] One week later, the ghoul's attorneys petitioned the court to arrest judgment because of his age. The court denied the request, and Hamp was given a week to prepare for prison.

On the way to Michigan City, West "stood the trip well and did not complain about anything except he would have been better satisfied if he had not been forced to wear handcuffs."[517] When the ghoul arrived in prison, "West immediately became an object of interest. He disliked very much the attention he attracted, but said nothing."[518] It's unclear if the Marion County charges still stood at the time, but it didn't matter. West died of stomach cancer in prison one year later. He was buried at Crown Hill Cemetery, where he remains interred to this day…presumably.

CHAPTER 14

AFTERMATH

After West, no other body snatcher in the ring faced a jury. Ruckelshaus dropped the charges against all other suspects or simply chose not to prosecute. With the exception of Joseph Alexander, no other medical school anatomist ever faced a jury.

However, everyday Hoosiers didn't easily forget Alexander's ghoulish activities even if prosecutors did. In November 1903, Alexander and his wife were walking to board a train at Fisher's Station when "they were attacked, dozens of eggs being thrown at them, several reaching their target."[519] Despite the public's ire, Alexander's lawyers moved to dismiss all charges against their client in April 1905, which the court granted. Forever a free man, Alexander later became the plant physician at Citizen Gas Company.

He died on December 3, 1925, from lobar pneumonia and was buried, perhaps purposefully, in an unmarked grave at Crown Hill Cemetery. There was no obituary for the doctor that I could find, but the Aetna Life Insurance Company took out a strange ad on December 7, 1925, proclaiming that Alexander's widow, Julia, received "a check for $3,000 covering the amount of life insurance provided in the mutual group insurance plan."

Dr. William Molt also went on to have a career as a physician, post-graverobbing. During most of 1903, Molt was conveniently away from Indianapolis, studying bronchology in New York City. He returned in September well after the trials[520] but made ghoulish headlines again two years later:

Five bodies in a state of decomposition, corpses used for dissecting purposes, was the ghastly find small boys made in the old building until recently occupied by the Eclectic Medical College, at Washington and Oriental streets, yesterday.[521]

Molt, who in 1905 worked at the Physio-Medical College, blamed the graduating senior class, saying that "the bodies had been used by that institution and the fact that they had not been removed sooner was a neglect of duty."[522] Molt's past apparently didn't raise any eyebrows because in 1929 he became a staff bronchologist at the city's General Hospital.[523] Before his retirement in 1953, Molt had served similar roles at Methodist and St. Vincent Hospitals. He died on January 12, 1958.[524]

Dr. Frank Wright, perhaps capitalizing on his writing experience as "Wallace Simms," founded the *Journal of Liberal Medicine* in 1904, serving as the publication's editor.[525] One year later, he entered into a public row with the Eclectic Medical Association, which charged the ghoul "of gross and unbecoming conduct, unworthy of a man seeking to enjoy the high honor and title of physician."[526] Several association members accused Wright and two others of "using the little handful of men and the name of the organization for their own advancement and for selfish ends."[527] Wright would go on to run a private practice for most of his career. He's listed in the 1920 *Polk Directory* with an office in the Pythian Building. He died on February 15, 1934, and was buried in his hometown of Salem, Indiana.

Adolph Asch, the well-known city police detective, retired from the force in 1914 after falling ill. Asch, a Jewish immigrant from Alsace-Lorraine, first arrived in the United States in 1882. He made his way to Indianapolis in 1885 and worked as a guard at the Marion County Workhouse. Three years later, Asch joined the city's metropolitan police department, eventually earning the rank of captain in 1906. He died of pneumonia in 1914 at the age of fifty-seven and is buried at the Indianapolis Hebrew Congregation Cemetery.[528]

Asch's partner, Chauncey Manning, also had an illustrious career as an Indianapolis police officer. He first joined the force in 1898 as a beat cop, later becoming a bicycle patrolman in 1901. According to his obituary, he achieved every rank over his career, with the exception of chief. He was promoted to detective in the wake of the graverobbing cases.[529] At his death, Manning was remembered as an "expert in the matter of questioning prisoners."[530] Instead of the usual third degree, Manning deployed a sort of quaint Hoosierism when questioning suspects.

Soldiers and Sailors Monument, late nineteenth or early twentieth century. *Library of Congress.*

If fellow detectives failed to get anywhere in questioning, they would suggest "Old Man Manning have a try."[531] Manning would then enter the interrogation room and sink "his great bulk back in a creaking chair, his chin drawn down on his chest." He'd let out a long sigh after staring for a few minutes at the suspect. Then, as calmly as possible, Manning would ask, "Son, where do you go to church?"

Whatever the answer, the detective would reply back, "Well, son, that's too bad, too bad. If you haven't anyone else to tell your troubles to and to help you out, you'd better tell 'em to us and let us try." At this point in questioning, Manning would deploy what he called the "psychological pipe." An excerpt from his obit illustrates perhaps just how he was able to get so much information from the ghouls:

> *The first few minutes of any interview with a violator were passed in dead silence as* [Manning] *with painful slowness, glancing sadly at the prisoner all the time, would carefully and meticulously load that old pipe,*

wadding every crumb of tobacco into the bowl and squeezing it down with a thumb. There would be a few irrelevant drawled questions and then another long pause as the hunt for a match began. Punctuating his slow search in every impossible pocket with gossipy questions as to the prisoner's parents, his family and how long he had lived in this vicinity, he at length would find the match and talk while it burned down to his fingers. Then he would have to hunt for another one or borrow one from the prisoner.[532]

The suspect, perhaps frustrated to the point of exhaustion, would lend the detective a match:

When the pipe was lit it generally went out after two puffs because the tobacco had been so tightly packed. Then for long minutes, Manning would knock it against his heel and carefully examine it for particles of remaining tobacco. He proceeded to clean his pipe slowly, asking small questions here and there. Then he'd ask for another match, the bowl was too packed, then the whole process would repeat.[533]

Questioning would go on for hours, Manning gleaning little bits of information as the suspect was irritated and distracted by the pipe. He "was probably the most expert in the matter of questioning prisoners ever known in Indianapolis. He was successful in almost every case in eliciting a frank and full confession from guilty culprits."[534] Manning retired from the IPD in 1928 and served as the head of the Indiana State Bureau of Criminal Investigation. He died in 1932 from heart disease and was buried at Crown Hill Cemetery.

Eugene Buehler, the secretary of the city board of health who may have threatened Ruckelshaus in 1902, would go on to serve as the editor of the *Indiana Medical Journal*. According to his obituary, he was also "a lieutenant in the sanitary corps in the Spanish-American war and a major in the world war."[535] He later moved to Texas and died in 1930 from heart disease. His body was returned to Indianapolis and buried at Crown Hill Cemetery.[536]

John Ruckelshaus served as the Marion County prosecutor for two terms, which began in 1900. He maintained a private law practice when not in office and worked as a public defender. He was active in Republican politics and became a Marion County attorney twice, once in 1908 and again in 1922. He died at the age of seventy-three in 1946. He was buried, like so many others in this story, at Crown Hill Cemetery.[537]

JOHN C. RUCKELSHAUS
Prosecuting Attorney or States Attorney for the Nineteenth
Judicial District of Indiana

MARTIN M. HUGG
Attorney-at-Law

Left: John Ruckelshaus, Marion County prosecutor. *Library of Congress.*

Right: Martin Hugg, Alexander's lawyer. *Library of Congress.*

Ruckelshaus's courtroom opponents had similar careers. Cass Connaway first came to Indianapolis in 1891 to practice law. During the First World War, he served as the judge advocate general of the YMCA in France. He later became the secretary of the Buffalo Real Estate Board. Connaway died at the age of seventy in 1939 and was buried at West Point Cemetery in his hometown of Liberty, Indiana.[538]

Taylor Groninger also came to Indianapolis to practice law, arriving in the Circle City in 1899. He later became a deputy prosecutor and city attorney. An active member of the city's Republican Party, he maintained his own law practice until his death in 1958. Groninger is also buried at Crown Hill.[539]

Martin Hugg, Alexander's attorney, was a former Marion County deputy prosecutor and Indianapolis city attorney. Hugg maintained a private practice and was active in the Republican Party. He served as a state senator in the Indiana General Assembly in 1896 and again in 1904. He died in 1938 and was buried at Crown Hill Cemetery.[540]

Judge George Stubbs is most known for launching Indianapolis's Juvenile Court in 1903. He also served three terms on the bench of the Indianapolis Police Court in 1893, 1895 and in 1901. A Union army veteran, Stubbs was

CHARLES FRANKLIN COFFIN
Lawyer, General Counsel State Life Insurance Co.
President Indianapolis, Greenwood & Franklin Railroad Co.

Left: George Stubbs in 1897, police court judge. *Library of Congress*.

Right: Charles Coffin, special judge appointed for Cantrell's trial. *Library of Congress*.

deaf in one ear and lost an arm in a hunting accident in 1899. He was hit and killed by an interurban car in 1911 and buried at Crown Hill Cemetery.[541]

Judge Fremont Alford, another prominent Indianapolis attorney, "had played an outstanding part in the legal profession in Indianapolis approximately a half century. He retired from the criminal bench in 1907 after having served as" judge of the Marion County Criminal Court for twelve years.[542] He, too, was buried at Crown Hill Cemetery.

Charles Coffin, the special judge with the apropos name presiding over Cantrell's trial, later became president of the State Life Insurance Company and was elected president of the Indianapolis Chamber of Commerce three times.[543] He died of a heart attack at the age of seventy-nine in 1935 and, you guessed it, was buried at Crown Hill Cemetery.

Cantrell's fellow ghouls also made headlines over the years. Sam Martin was arrested in 1911 and charged with running a gambling house in the Sixth Ward Colored Workers Club.[544] After Isom Donnell was released from prison in 1906, "he returned to this city, where he made his home since. He was employed upon his return by Frank W. Ward, a saloon keeper on West Sixteenth Street."[545] He died of lung disease in 1906 and was buried at Crown Hill Cemetery.

Left: Isom Donnell's mugshot photo from 1903. *Indiana State Archives*.

Right: Sol Grady's mugshot photo from 1903. *Indiana State Archives*.

Sol Grady was released from prison at the same time as Donnell. Grady's name appears frequently in early twentieth-century Indy newspapers. He was arrested in 1915 after shooting Frank Bridges over a horse. The *Indianapolis Star* reported that "Grady escaped following the shooting. Bridges received two bullet wounds in the right arm and a third bullet pierced his stomach. He has almost entirely recovered. Grady is said to be a Democratic worker in the colored section of the city."[546] He apparently escaped prosecution, having "been protected in his crime by all the artifaces known to the machine politician."[547]

In November 1918, Grady was charged with operating a speakeasy.[548] He was fined $100 and spent thirty days in jail.[549] He was arrested again the next year "on a charge of keeping a gambling house" at 872 Massachusetts Avenue.[550] Grady was found guilty, fined $10 and spent ten days in county jail. Taylor Groninger was his counsel.[551] Grady died of acute nephritis at the age of sixty-two in 1932.

William Jones suffered a mental health crisis in prison and was transferred to a hospital. The *Star* reported in 1906 that "Jones is insane, having spent the last year of his term of imprisonment in the asylum at the prison."[552] Jones seemed haunted to his fellow inmates: "He sits quietly in the corner shunning the other prisoners," who seem "to regard him with a feeling of superstitious aversion."[553]

I couldn't find much about the lives of the other cast of characters in this story, post-graverobbing. The details of their later lives remain buried deep in the historical record, if at all.

However, the biggest mystery is what became of Rufus Cantrell.

CHAPTER 15

WHERE IS RUFUS CANTRELL?

I n August 1903, Cantrell made a series of false confessions, or perhaps he disclosed information about crimes that investigators did not find credible. Cantrell professed to being an accomplice in the murder of Walter Johnson, who some years prior had been robbed and beaten to death in downtown Indianapolis.[554] Cantrell also admitted to witnessing the murder of an Indianapolis policeman named John Watterson in 1893 and a man named Claude who was "enticed to Beech Grove, where a quarrel was picked and he was beaten to death with a club."[555] He made a similar claim about a murder of a Philadelphia librarian named William Wilson.

Cantrell also confessed to being present at the murder of a man named "Jim" who was blackmailing Dr. William Molt. Jim was stabbed in a buggy and "the body turned over to an Indianapolis doctor who in turn gave it to another Indianapolis physician"[556] for dissection.

In this latest string of jailhouse confessions, Cantrell also reiterated that he knew what happened to Carrie Selvage. He told Joseph Byers, the outgoing superintendent of Jeffersonville Penitentiary, that he was riding back from a job with a fellow ghoul one night when the pair noticed a disheveled woman "coming toward us. She was bareheaded and wore a loose blue wrapper. She was of medium size, slender, white, and had brown hair. This hair I later sold to a milliner near the corner of Washington and Pennsylvania streets."[557]

According to Cantrell, this woman was speaking gibberish and asked for the ghouls to take her home. She was kidnapped instead and taken to a Hamilton County house, "where this woman was kept for several weeks. The woman's name, I believe, was Selvage." After her disappearance made press, Cantrell's unnamed associate killed her with chloroform and buried her body in an empty grave at Union Chapel Cemetery.[558]

No one really believed Cantrell. Joseph Selvage, Carrie's brother, said "he considered every statement made by Cantrell a downright lie."[559] Indianapolis police captain Samuel Gerber was tasked with investigating the claims. He told the *Indianapolis Star* that Cantrell "has lied so much and so many of his stories have been found to be fiction that we can have no confidence in what he says."[560] Gerber also spread a rumor of his own: "When he was up here to

Rufus Cantrell's mugshot photo from 1903. *Indiana State Archives.*

testify [in West's trial], he told detective Kurtz that he intended to go back to Jeffersonville and make a full confession that would clear up a number of murders and then commit suicide."[561]

The IPD conducted a small investigation, which included some intense questioning of the ghoul Walter Williams, but nothing came from it. Detectives found no evidence to support any of Cantrell's claims. The new superintendent at the Jeffersonville reformatory, W.H. Whittaker, moved to gag Rufus's press interaction. Whittaker believed "it will be best for the institution and best for the general public if the negro ghoul is kept at hard labor in the prison foundry, and secluded from those seeing sensational stories from him. It is feared that his appetite for notoriety will prove insatiable."[562]

RUFUS WILLIAM CANTRELL IS a bit of an enigma. There isn't enough documented information to provide a thorough biography. We also don't have Cantrell's interpretation of these events. He told reporters during West's trial that he was writing a book about his life and had more than 250 pages completed.[563] Even if this was true, the manuscript has been lost. Cantrell's life story in the historical record is simply limited to a few vital documents and some fragmentary newspaper articles.

The only other relevant information that I could find about Cantrell came many years later from a doctor by the name of Goethe Link. In 1977, Link wrote an article in the *Indiana Medical History Quarterly* about the early history

Rufus Cantrell's mugshot photo from 1903. *Indiana State Archives.*

of Indianapolis's medical schools. The author reminisced that Cantrell was "the toughest man I've ever seen—very loquacious and full of braggadocio." Link also wrote that Cantrell was one of three body snatchers operating in Marion County at the time, but was "the most active and the most ruthless." In 1902, Link had worked with C.L. Durham at Central Medical and often met with Cantrell as he delivered corpses. The ghoul would often linger "after delivering a body and [entertained] me with tales of his graverobbing." Link even boldly asserted that Durham had visited Cantrell in jail and threatened to see him hanged for his crimes. Cantrell never mentioned Durham or Link in any of his testimony.[564]

Cantrell's race also played a significant part in how this story was covered and how Hoosiers interpreted it. Rufus wasn't a moral man, but he was no less culpable in graverobbing than the doctors, internists, sextons, undertakers and students at the medical colleges, not to mention all the other white ghouls resurrecting across central Indiana. All but West avoided legal repercussions for their crimes. Cantrell and his crew of graverobbers were easy scapegoats in a racist society because they were Black.

Yet despite these limitations in source material, there's enough information to construct a general timeline of Cantrell's life, at least until he disappears completely from the historical record around 1920.

Rufus William Cantrell was born on April 3 in either 1876, 1879, 1880 or 1881 in Gallatin, Tennessee, to Sarah (Sallie) and Rufus Cantrell Sr. The future graverobber had several siblings and half siblings. After Rufus senior died, some of the Cantrells moved to Indianapolis in the mid-1890s, where Junior worked several jobs including as a chauffeur. We know this because he was fined in early 1897 for driving a transfer wagon on the wrong side of the street.[565]

That same year, the future ghoul enlisted in the U.S. Army, serving as a private in Company A of the Twenty-Fourth Infantry Division. Cantrell was stationed in Utah at Fort Douglas. His name appears in the U.S. Army Registry of Enlistments as Rufus W. Cantrell of Indianapolis, hometown Gallatin, Tennessee. He's listed as twenty-one years of age in 1897, and his occupation was "undertaker."

A busy Washington Street in 1902. *From* The Journal Handbook of Indianapolis, *Indianapolis–Marion County Public Library.*

Rufus was either discharged or placed on leave in 1898 with a surgeon's certificate of disability. He married Ophilia Franklin on October 24, 1898, and the couple had at least one child. In 1899, he's listed in Polk's *Indianapolis City Directory* as living with his mother at 351 West Fourteenth Street and working as a porter. From 1900 to 1903, his permanent address is listed in the directories as 613 Fayette Street. The 1900 federal census lists him at the same place.

In October of that year, Cantrell was the president of the Bookwalter Colored Club, a Black Republican political group supporting Charles Bookwalter's candidacy for mayor of Indianapolis.[566] His political loyalties appeared to have been split between the parties, however, because he was beaten in a saloon later that month for "declaring his intention to vote for Bryan," as in William Jennings Bryan, Democratic candidate for president. Cantrell was fined five dollars for starting the fight and was described in the newspaper report as an undertaker's assistant.[567]

In February 1901, Cantrell was arrested for shooting a man along the canal. According to the *Journal*, Cantrell got into an epic argument with Emanuel Roach and Garfield Buckner. Rufus was "accused by Roach of being a coward and unable to fight a 'good man' without a revolver and club."[568] Another version of the story had it that the ghouls were arguing over debt. Whatever the truth, Cantrell shot him "several times, one bullet striking Roach in the forehead, but doing little injury."[569]

During his 1903 state incarceration, Cantrell served as a cook and later in the foundry at the Indiana State Prison in Jeffersonville. In November of that year, he was transferred to the state prison in Michigan City.[570] Rumors circulated a year later that Rufus had gone insane and was "dying of typhoid fever at Michigan City prison"[571] and that he was "unconscious for nearly a week."[572] These reports turned out to be false. "There is no foundation for the story that Rufus Cantrell…is a raving maniac in the prison hospital, due to typhoid fever," the *Muncie Morning Star* reported. "Cantrell was recently in the hospital for two days because of a slight indisposition. He is fat and hearty, and daily at work."[573]

Cantrell was denied parole for a third time in June 1905. The *Indianapolis Star* wrote that he was "employed on the stone contract in the prison and is regarded as a model prisoner."[574] Cantrell even had a job, if you can believe it, making state grave markers. "Confinement does not seem to impair his health and he seems to enjoy making tombstones."[575]

Rufus was granted parole four years later in 1909. The *Fort Wayne Sentinel* wrote that a member of the parole board "said that Cantrell had been a model prisoner, and that the authorities feared, if he were kept longer in prison, his mind would be permanently affected."[576] Cantrell offered to tell the board more information about graverobbing, but they "did not seek this information."[577]

One of Cantrell's parole conditions barred him from living in Indianapolis. The former ghoul settled in nearby Anderson instead and got a job as a stoker at the American Steel and Wire Mill, where "his employers give him credit as being faithful of duty."[578] He appeared in a Madison County courtroom later that September, but this time as a victim. Cantrell was working one day at the mill, minding his own, when a coworker named Theodore Price attacked him. Price was fired and charged with assault and battery.[579] Later that year, just before Christmas 1909, Rufus married Hattie Patterson in the "home of Mr. and Mrs. Patterson, parents of the bride. The Rev. B.J. Coleman, of the African M.E. church, performed the ceremony."[580]

Cantrell was never far from controversy. His name appears again in papers mid-August 1910. The former ghoul planned to appear in vaudeville stage performances across east-central Indiana. The *Muncie Morning Star* wrote that "he is to go on the stage and is heralded in newspaper advertisements and on billboards as 'Cantrell, the King of the Ghouls'" and will deliver "a

SYNDICATE OF DEATH REVEALED BY C

"Sign of the Cross" Secret Token of Band of Desperadoes.

MURDER DONE BY A SYSTEM

Bodies of Victims Sold to Demonstrators of Anatomy at $30 Each.

DETECTIVES ARE AMAZED

Chief of the Gang Sells Sweetheart's Body Without Identifying It Until Bargain Is Carried Out.

CANTRELL'S HEADQUARTERS

COUNTY

INDIANAPOLIS, Ind., Saturday.

THIS is the sign of the cross, secret token of a band of desperadoes whose operations were long conducted with impunity:—

R. | W.

C. |

R. W. C. are the initials of Rufus William Cantrell, the recognized leader of the gang, who is now serving an indeterminate sentence of from three to ten years in the Indiana State Reformatory, at Jeffersonville. Originally arrested upon the comparatively trivial charge of obtaining a small sum of money by false pretences, Cantrell was locked up in the Marion County Jail here a few months ago. The serious charge of robbing graves was then made against him, and, as the evidence accumulated showing that he had been regularly engaged in the traffic of bodies he was popularly dubbed "King of the Ghouls."

He has now confessed that he was the controlling spirit in a murder syndicate such as was never before exposed in the United States. For petty gain person after person was lured to death. The small hoardings of a crippled mendicant, the meagre savings of a migratory colored butler, the pocket money of a foolish white youth who had displayed some greenbacks while drinking in a resort of negroes—these were the primary motives for murder in three instances that appear to have been typical of many others—first there was the money to be obtained from the victim and then the dead body had a recognized commercial value.

Cantrell and his gang had the effrontery to sell to medical colleges bodies of persons whom they had killed, apparently indifferent to the fact that the anatomical demonstrators with whom they dealt should have been able to discover at once that murder had been done.

The old adage of honor among thieves cannot be applied to grave robbers. A member of Cantrell's gang died, and his body quickly found its way to the dissecting table. The body of another member's wife was sold to a college, and finally

prime mover, it seems to have fallen far short of the number of murders actually committed. Evidence of new crimes is accumulating. It is a black record.

"Murder, murder, murder everywhere!" exclaimed Detective Asch this morning. "The evidence is all inextricably intertwined. Each time I try to learn facts in one case another case bobs up and I am led off in another direction. There can be no doubt that the murders were committed, and not alone those that Cantrell has acknowledge, but many others which he has tried to conceal. In some instances the trail leads far from Indianapolis. You will observe that he confines his official confession to murders within the city limits, while the fact seems to be that most of his crimes were committed outside. Some of these he has been most anxious to hide, as the facts at hand indicate that he alone was guilty and that consequently it would be useless for him to attempt to shift the blame to others."

To use Detective Asch's graphic expression, Cantrell's admissions came as junk—that is to say, by stray bits, without any seeming connection. The first murder mystery that was solved by his aid was that of Doc Lung, a Chinese laundry man, who had been found dead with his head nearly severed from his body. Some of Doc Lung's fellow countrymen were arrested on suspicion, but as no proof could be obtained against them, they were eventually released.

While Cantrell was in the county jail here awaiting trial it occurred to Manning to question him about this murder, which had passed out of public notice.

"Tell me what you know about that Doc Lung case, Rufus," said the detective, nonchalantly, after a short chat about other matters.

"What for you ask me that?" said Cantrell angrily. "You should not ask me such things."

Anger Causes Confession.

A typical full-page spread of the case, from the *New York Herald*, August 16, 1903. *Library of Congress.*

ESSION OF MOST DARING OF GHOULS

MT. JACKSON CEMETERY

CENTRAL MEDICAL COLLEGE

Mystery of Wealthy Girl's Disappearance Cleared After Months of Searching.

FIRST ABDUCTED AND THEN SLAIN

Her Hair Sold and Her Body Interred in a Grave Previously Despoiled.

OTHER CRIMES TRACED

Justice Hampered by the Untimely Publication of Cantrell's Sworn Statement to Prison Warden.

before any step is taken before the Grand Jury we must have something very much more substantial than that man's word. There is a very strong prejudice against him, and I understand that he realizes it and that he has said that if he ever gets out of jail he will not attempt to return to Indianapolis. Indeed, he feels that it would not be safe for him to come here. In a trial many persons would be inclined to disregard entirely anything that he might say."

Since the change in administration at the reformatory things have gone harder for Cantrell. He has been transferred from light work to the heaviest labor in the iron castings department, and the new superintendent has announced that the ghoul will have less opportunity hereafter to talk for publication.

The crime of grave robbing, which first brought Cantrell into national notoriety, is believed by many intelligent persons to have been fostered by the law as it then stood in Indiana. The only bodies that the medical and dental colleges here were entitled to obtain were those of paupers and prisoners in this county which were unclaimed by relatives. There are usually from six hundred to eight hundred medical students in Indianapolis, and the dozen bodies obtained legitimately did not begin to supply the demand.

There was a shortage of from seventy-five to one hundred bodies a year. The demonstrators were glad enough to get any that were offered to them at the standard price of $30, delivered, and no questions asked. From time to time there have been minor scandals about grave robbing, but they were quickly hushed until the stories of the wholesale desecration of cemeteries were made public last spring. Since then the old law has been changed and all paupers and criminals who die in the State are offered to the colleges for the cost of the shipment. It is said now that the colleges are so well supplied that offers of bodies from distant portions of the State are usually refused.

He begged her not to tell and she promised that she would not on one condition, that the body be removed at once, as she feared that innocent persons might be jeopardized by keeping the body of the murdered man where it lay. Martin then found Cantrell, and they engaged "Ed" Cousins to remove a barrel from the house in his transfer wagon. The barrel proved very heavy. It was taken to the Indiana Dental College. Cantrell admits that the barrel contained Jordan's body, for which he received $30.

"Sam" Martin does not admit that this version of the killing is correct, though he does not deny that he was present when Jordan was murdered. He says he reached the yard just in time to see Cantrell and "Ollie" Morton strike the fatal blows. He declares that he was asked by Cantrell and Morton the next morning to keep talking to the truck driver to prevent the man from becoming too inquisitive, but he would not even do that, and he left the partners in crime to take care of the body

Grave Robbery Not Illegal.

great lecture on his past horrible life."[581] This didn't sit well with Hoosiers, plus such a show would violate Cantrell's parole. An effort was made to shut the production down, which must have succeeded. I can't find any record of a performance.[582]

Cantrell might also have been pressured to leave town. In the 1910 census, he's listed as the spouse of Hattie Cantrell in Dayton, Ohio. It's not clear if he was living there at the time of the census, but he was by 1912. In that year, he returned to his old profession as a preacher.[583] People who knew Cantrell, as the *Muncie Evening Press* reported, said "that he has reformed and that he is doing much good among colored and whites of the underworld at Dayton."[584]

By September 1912, Cantrell was living in Mount Clemens, Michigan, and working as a cook for a crew of paving laborers. Cantrell was also pursuing political interests. The *Indianapolis Star* reported at the end of the month that "Cantrell is preparing to enter the field as a speaker for [Woodrow Wilson], beginning in Michigan."[585] He told a reporter that he spent his nights writing poetry.[586]

Cantrell moved back to Indianapolis in 1913 to stump for local candidates. The newspaper reports never mention the parole condition of not living in Indy—perhaps it had expired. Regardless, Cantrell was living a public life in Indianapolis during the fall 1913 campaign season, raising support for Joseph Bell, the Democratic candidate for mayor of Indianapolis. Bell's opponent was Charles Bookwalter, a Republican whom Cantrell once supported but now despised.

Rufus was working with several other Black Indianapolitans to drum up African American votes for Democratic candidates. The *Indianapolis News* wrote that "Cantrell, Hubbard, and Banks are busy trying to line up the colored voters for Bell. As a preliminary step they held a meeting above a saloon in Indiana Avenue last Friday night…about twenty-five colored men are said to have attended."[587]

In one speech, Cantrell said that "the political grave of Charles A. Bookwalter and Dr. William H. Johnson will be dug today."[588] Bell's campaign saw Rufus as a man "of influence and power among a certain class of negroes and their support was welcome, although in private."[589] Bell didn't want to look *too* chummy with a former body snatcher, even if the former ghoul could drum up votes. As to Cantrell's shift of political party, "he explained that he came a convert to the Democratic party after Governor Hanly refused to pardon or parole him, but told his mother if he had a rope he would use it to hang him."[590]

At a major rally mid-month, Cantrell leaned in hard on his public graverobbing image, declaring "that the only mistake he ever made in handling the 'dead ones' was in failing to hook Bookwalter himself."[591] He then proceeded to compare Bell to Moses and Abraham Lincoln.

Bookwalter was amused with his opponent's choice of supporters, telling a crowd, "We are going to put Mr. Bell so far in the ground that even his friend, Rufus Cantrell, will not be able to dig him out."[592] Bookwalter wasn't speaking of reality, though, as he lost the election by a wide margin.

Cantrell appeared again in Indianapolis newspapers in early 1914. He was arrested for operating a speakeasy and gambling house. In police court, Cantrell argued that he was simply storing liquor at the Colored Men's Democratic Club at 416 Indiana Avenue; he just hadn't had the chance yet to move it. Judge Deery didn't buy it. He fined Cantrell fifty dollars and sentenced him to thirty days in jail,[593] although he was acquitted of operating a gambling house a week later.[594] Rufus appealed his conviction to the criminal court, but it would be over a year before the case was heard. Rufus could afford bail this time and stayed out of jail to await the appeal's outcome.

Mid-April, the *News* reported that Cantrell was at odds with the Bell administration, as the new mayor "loaded the street cleaning department with Republican colored men and ignored Democrats who had worked for Bell." Nonetheless, Cantrell "affirmed an abiding faith in Mayor Bell."[595]

Hattie divorced Rufus in 1915. The *Dayton Daily News* printed a legal notice: "Rufus Cantrell, whose place of residence is unknown, will take notice that Hattie Cantrell" was suing "for a divorce from said Rufus Cantrell, restoration to her maiden name of Hattie Patterson, and for equitable relief, upon the grounds of gross neglect of duty and habitual drunkenness and willful absence for more than three years last past, and extreme cruelty."[596]

Back in Indianapolis, Rufus's speakeasy appeal was called in criminal court, but he didn't show. The court issued a warrant for his arrest. No one at the time really knew where he was. The *Indianapolis Star* printed a rumor that "Cantrell, the last heard from, was preaching in Flint, Michigan."[597]

The gossip proved true, as Cantrell was indeed sermonizing in Michigan in late 1915. He also found love again and remarried, this time to May McConnell.[598] The couple had united across the border in Windsor, Canada. The newlyweds were leading members of a religious organization known as the Charity Army of America. At some point, Cantrell fled Flint with May after an unfavorable newspaper report charged the Charity Army of fleecing its flock. The couple resettled in Detroit and partnered with Reverend

Albert Johnson to reopen the mission. During a revival service, Cantrell was arrested "on a charge of assault and battery preferred by a woman who had been attending."[599]

After learning of the accusations in Flint, Detroit police added the charge of grand larceny and closed Cantrell's mission, prohibiting him or any of "his associates from collecting money under the guise of charity."[600] Another associate named Edward Gowdy was also arrested. During the subsequent trial, prosecutors proved that Cantrell, "while conducting services in the Gospel Praise Mission, is alleged to have preached as a cloak for his thefts. It was brought out that Gowdy would 'frisk' the pockets of men and women when they were on their knees listening to Cantrell pray."[601]

Apparently, Cantrell and Gowdy had a falling out. Soon after their arrest Rufus claimed that "Gowdy, with several negro companions, abducted Miss Selvage, imprisoned her in the basement of an old house for several days, where she was mistreated, then murdered her and her body was sold to a medical college."[602] Rufus "declared Gowdy killed the woman and that he, Cantrell, later sold the body."[603]

Gowdy denied any involvement in Carrie Selvage's disappearance. The information was forwarded to the Indianapolis police, who just rolled their eyes and dismissed it out of hand. Cantrell's story didn't help, as both men were found guilty and sentenced to two years in the Michigan Penitentiary at Marquette.

Gowdy died of a heart attack while in prison. Cantrell served out his term and was released in 1917. A Detroit directory from that year lists "R.W. Cantrell" living in that city with several family members at 3066 East Grand Boulevard, employed as an autoworker. However, I suspect that the directory information was collected or printed before Cantrell's arrest.

On September 12, 1918, Cantrell filed his registration card at the local draft board in Marquette with information suggesting he lived there. He noted the following: his name was Rufus William Cantrell; he was thirty-nine years old; his birthday was April 3, 1879; he lived at the Merchant's Hotel in Marquette; and he was employed as a cement worker at Lake Superior and Ishpeming Railroad's roundhouse in the city. He listed his mother, Sarah Cantrell, as his nearest relative, living at 715 Lafayette Street in Indianapolis.[604] Rufus or a clerk marked that he was African American, tall and stout, with brown eyes and black hair.[605]

Cantrell vanishes from the record after this. At least, I can't find any other credible documented information as to his whereabouts. He doesn't appear in the 1920 or 1930 census, nor in Detroit or Indianapolis city directories.

Several other Rufus Cantrells lived at the same time in the United States, but they don't match the body snatcher's race or age. Rufus simply disappears from the historical record after 1918.

Carrie Selvage, however, did not. In late April 1920, "an old-time mystery, caused by the disappearance in Indianapolis twenty years ago of Carrie T. Selvage…was solved today by the finding of the skeleton of a woman in an attic of a brick building at 1333 North Capitol avenue." The brick building in 1920 was an apartment complex, but at the time of Selvage's disappearance, it was the Union States Hospital, where Selvage had been institutionalized. It seems that she never disappeared at all, but rather escaped into part of the attic and just died there, or so the story went.

In a hidden attic recess, workmen found the skeleton in a blue dress sitting in a corner, "her skull had fallen to the floor and the bones of the upper part of the skeleton were leaning against the wall."[606] The coroner said "it was impossible to determine whether the woman was carried to the attic by some one or whether she went to the place on her own accord and starved herself to death." The skeleton's dress and slippers matched what Selvage was wearing at the time of her disappearance. Her brothers, saddened but perhaps relieved in a way, buried the remains at Crown Hill Cemetery.

EPILOGUE

I n mid-March 1904, the *Elwood Daily Record* wrote that "for a year there has not been a grave robbery case in Indiana." But this wasn't to last. Two months later, the *Indianapolis News* reported that "it is the belief of many persons in and around Fisher's Station that cemeteries in the southern part of Hamilton County are again being robbed of their dead."[607] And as the prologue to this book demonstrates, attempts were made in DeSoto at the end of the year.

Body snatching did eventually die out in Indiana after the trials, but not because of them. Modern embalming methods allowed for medical schools to stockpile cadavers. As Suzanne Shultz wrote in her 1992 book *Body Snatching*, "Cadaver storage and preservation improved thus drawing to a close the necessities of hasty dissection before putrefaction occurred. Cadavers obtained from legal sources could be accumulated over the period of time when classes were not in session."[608]

According to Shultz, in the early 1900s "accounts of body snatching received less attention in newspapers. Possibly reporters thought that all bodies used by medical schools were obtained from legal sources. Perhaps grave robbing expertise had reached such a state of perfection that it was difficult to detect. In any case, with legal sources of supply on the rise because of revision in state laws, prices of illegal merchandise would have declined."[609]

Such is the way body snatching ended in the United States: with the advent of new technology—not a shift from a resurrected morality but from

DISTURB NOT THE DEAD

What should be the punishment of men who fiendishly make merchandise of the dead?

Editorial cartoon from the *Indianapolis Journal*, October 1, 1902. *Hoosier State Chronicles.*

the banality of a changed market. I do wonder, though, how much "illegal merchandise" was really taken out of the ground in the late nineteenth century? How many graves lie empty still across the Hoosier state?

NOTES

Prologue

1. "Enraged Farmers Fired on Ghouls," *Muncie Morning Star*, December 6, 1904, 7.
2. Ibid.
3. "Battle Between Brothers of Dead Minister and Four Ghouls," *Courier Journal*, December 6, 1904, 6.
4. Ibid.
5. "Work of the Graverobbers," *Indianapolis News*, December 7, 1904, 15.
6. "Guard for the Graveyard," *Huntington Weekly Herald*, December 8, 1904, 4.

Introduction

7. See Historic Indianapolis, "Rufus Cantrell, Intruder in the Dust," https://historicindianapolis.com/rufus-cantrell-intruder-in-the-dust.
8. See Dawn Mitchell, "The Business of Body Snatching in Indianapolis," *Indy Star*, May 1, 2016, https://www.indystar.com/story/news/2016/05/01/business-body-snatching-indianapolis/83544696.
9. See Hamilton East Public Library, "Grave Robbing in Fishers, Part I," https://www.hepl.lib.in.us/grave-robbing-in-fishers-part-1.
10. See Lindsey Beckley, "'King of Ghouls' Rufus Cantrell and Grave-Robbing in Indianapolis," *Indianapolis History Blog*, October 31, 2020,

https://blog.history.in.gov/king-of-ghouls-rufus-cantrell-grave-robbing-in-indianapolis.

11. See Talking Hoosier History, "Rufus Cantrell: King of Ghouls," October 28, 2020, https://talkinghoosierhistory.libsyn.com/rufus-cantrell-king-of-ghouls.

Chapter 1

12. "Ghouls in the Graveyard," *Indianapolis Journal*, September 20, 1902, 3.
13. Central College was in the midst of opening its new facility on North Senate Avenue, but this was not operational in September 1902.
14. "Ghouls in the Graveyard," 3.
15. Ibid.
16. All quotes from "Ghouls in the Graveyard," 3.
17. "Body Is Recovered," *Indianapolis Journal*, September 22, 1902, 12.
18. Ibid.
19. Ibid.
20. Ibid.
21. Ibid.
22. Ibid.
23. Ibid.
24. Ibid.
25. "Grave Robbing Gang Captured," *Indianapolis News*, September 29, 1902, 2.
26. Ibid.
27. The papers spell his name "Gronninger," while the 1902 *Polk Directory* spells it "Groninger"; I've used the latter spelling.
28. "Grave Robbing Gang Captured," 2.
29. The papers used the words *negro* and *colored* to describe African Americans. This is certainly othering, but the words weren't considered pejorative at the time. I'll quote the papers as they wrote the story, but in my own writing, I use *Black* or *African American*.
30. "Grave Robbing Gang Captured," 1.
31. Ibid.
32. Ibid.
33. Ibid.
34. Ibid.
35. Ibid.

36. Ibid.
37. Ibid.
38. Ibid.
39. Ibid.
40. Ibid.
41. Ibid.
42. Ibid.
43. Ibid.
44. Ibid.

Chapter 2

45. Michael Sappol, *A Traffic of Dead Bodies: Anatomy and Embodied Social Identity in Nineteenth-Century America* (Princeton, NJ: Princeton University Press, 2002), 5.
46. Ibid.
47. Suzanne Shultz, *Body Snatching: The Robbing of Graves for the Education of Physicians in Early Nineteenth Century America* (Jefferson, NC: McFarland Press, 2005), 18.
48. Sappol, *Traffic of Dead Bodies*, 4.
49. Ibid., 17.
50. Ibid., 18.
51. "Grave Robbing," *Indianapolis News*, December 4, 1873, 4.
52. Ibid.
53. "Further Particulars," *Indiana State Sentinel*, October 27, 1874, 1.
54. "He Wants to Stop It," *Indianapolis News*, December 29, 1874, 3.
55. "City News," *Indianapolis News*, December 20, 1875, 4.
56. "Legislative Summary," *Indiana State Sentinel*, February 2, 1875, 4.
57. "Only Absolute Safety," *Indianapolis News*, December 14, 1875, 2.
58. "Body Snatching," *Fort Wayne Daily Gazette*, April 23, 1877, 1.
59. "Grave Robbing," *Huntington Democrat*, November 14, 1878, 3.
60. *Indiana State Sentinel*, January 8, 1870, 4.
61. Ibid.
62. "State News," *Indianapolis Journal*, March 1, 1890, 2.
63. "General State News," *Indianapolis News*, March 10, 1890, 1.
64. "Indiana and Illinois News," *Indianapolis Journal*, March 1, 1890, 2.
65. *Indiana State Sentinel*, April 8, 1891, 8.
66. "General State News," *Indianapolis News*, June 23, 1890, 1.

67. "Charged with Grave-Robbing," *Indianapolis Journal*, June 22, 1890, 1.
68. "Late State News," *Indianapolis News*, August 6, 1890, 2.
69. "Janitor Arrested," *Indianapolis News*, January 20, 1892, 2.
70. Ibid.
71. "Jeff Garrigus Acquitted," *Indianapolis Journal*, April 23, 1892, 5.
72. "'Ghoul' in a Jail," *Indianapolis Journal*, October 18, 1894, 5.
73. "Jeff Garrigus Arrested," *Indianapolis News*, February 14, 1898, 9.
74. In local lore, this is a haunted cemetery known as "100 Steps."
75. "Grave Robbery at Cloverland," *Indianapolis News*, November 19, 1892, 1.
76. "Greenwood Grave Robbed," *Indianapolis News*, December 26, 1894, 2.
77. "Bodies for Dissection," *Indianapolis News*, December 27, 1894, 5.
78. Ibid.
79. "Arrested for Grave Robbing," *Indianapolis Journal*, February 26, 1895, 2.
80. "Loaded with Nitro-Glycerine," *Indianapolis News*, August 15, 1895, 7.
81. "Those Grave Robbing Tools," *Indianapolis News*, September 26, 1900, 8.
82. "Drove Near Cemetery," *Indianapolis News*, September 25, 1900, 9.

Chapter 3

83. "Caught in the Web," *Indianapolis Journal*, October 1, 1902, 1.
84. Ibid.
85. "Bodies Spirited Away," *Indianapolis Journal*, October 1, 1902, 3.
86. "Caught in the Web," 3.
87. Ibid.
88. Ibid.
89. Ibid.
90. Ibid.
91. "Law's Strong Arm," *Indianapolis Journal*, October 2, 1902, 10.
92. "More Damage Suits," *Indianapolis News*, October 7, 1902, 1.
93. Ibid.
94. Ibid.
95. Ibid.
96. "Conference with Cantrell," *Indianapolis Journal*, October 6, 1902, 8.
97. "Graves Opened in Mt. Jackson," *Indianapolis News*, October 7, 1902, 1.
98. "Hunting for Bodies," *Indianapolis Journal*, October 3, 1902, 10.
99. Ibid.
100. "Visit to Graveyards," *Indianapolis Journal*, October 8, 1902, 7. Cantrell later denied the ice story.

101. "Louisville Bodies Seen," *Indianapolis Journal*, October 11, 1902, 10.

102. "Crown Hill Patrol," *Indianapolis Journal*, October 5, 1902, 20.

103. Ibid.

104. O.W. Crabs, "Beech Grove Cemetery Not Visited by Ghouls," *Muncie Morning Star*, October 11, 1902, 5.

105. "Bodies in Cold Storage," *Indianapolis Journal*, October 9, 1902, 10.

106. "Four Bodies Found," *Indianapolis Journal*, October 14, 1902, 10.

107. Ibid.

Chapter 4

108. "Corpses Given Up by Grave Robbers," *Muncie Star*, October 14, 1902, 6.

109. "Four Bodies Found," *Indianapolis Journal*, October 14, 1902, 10.

110. "Grand Jury Investigation," *Indianapolis Journal*, October 21, 1902, 8.

111. "Rufus Cantrell Tells Grand Jury His Story," *Indianapolis News*, October 14, 1902, 11.

112. Ibid.

113. Ibid.

114. "Cantrell's Papers Gone," *Indianapolis Journal*, October 17, 1902, 10.

115. "Want Simple Justice," *Indianapolis Journal*, October 19, 1902, 13.

116. Ibid.

117. Ibid.

118. Ibid.

119. Ibid.

120. "Grave Robber Inquiry," *Indianapolis Journal*, October 22, 1902, 3.

121. "Cantrell in Louisville," *Indianapolis Journal*, October 25, 1902, 1.

122. Ibid.

123. Ibid.

124. Ibid.

125. "Rufus Cantrell Tells Grand Jury His Story," *Indianapolis News*, October 14, 1902, 11.

126. Ibid.

127. "Find Body Amid Garbage," *Fort Wayne Sentinel*, October 21, 1902.

128. "Bodies Out of the Cellar," *Indianapolis Journal*, October 15, 1902, 12.

129. "Ghouls Are Indicted," *Indianapolis Journal*, October 26, 1902, 10.

130. Ibid., 4.

131. Ibid.

132. "Ghouls in Court," *Indianapolis Journal*, October 28, 1902, 1.
133. Ibid.
134. Ibid.
135. Ibid.

Chapter 5

136. "Get a White Ghoul," *Indianapolis Journal*, November 1, 1902, 10.
137. Ibid.
138. Ibid.
139. Ibid.
140. Ibid.
141. Ibid.
142. Ibid.
143. "Just for a Lark," *Indianapolis Journal*, November 2, 1902, 8.
144. Ibid.
145. Ibid.
146. "Ghastly Brand of Humor," *Indianapolis Journal*, November 4, 1902, 10.
147. Ibid.
148. "Graves Are Found Empty," *Indianapolis Journal*, November 8, 1902, 10.
149. Ibid.
150. Ibid.
151. Ibid.
152. Ibid.
153. "Moffett an Alleged Ghoul," *Indianapolis Journal*, November 12, 1902, 6.
154. Ibid.
155. "Men of Blood," *Indianapolis News*, January 25, 1879, 4.
156. Ibid.
157. Ibid.
158. "In Eternity," *Indianapolis News*, January 29, 1879, 1.
159. "Another Ghoul Caught," *Indianapolis Journal*, November 13, 1902, 10.
160. Ibid.
161. "More Graves Opened," *Indianapolis Journal*, November 12, 1902, 10.
162. Ibid.
163. Ibid.
164. "Farmer Stole Bodies," *Indianapolis Journal*, November 14, 1902, 1.
165. "Murder," *The Ledger*, November 25, 1881, 1.
166. Ibid.

167. Ibid. West identified himself in 1881 as a farmer; "Murder," 1.

168. Ibid.

169. A wooden mallet used to open a cask of booze.

170. Ibid.

171. "Murder," 1.

172. Ibid.

173. Ibid.

174. Ibid.

175. Ibid.

176. Ibid.

177. "Additional Local," *Ledger*, December 9, 1881, 8. This was reenacted as the "Battle of Mudsock" in 2019; see https://www.battleofmudsock.com.

178. "Criminal Court," *Indianapolis Journal*, April 1, 1891, 6.

179. "Avenged," *Hamilton County Democrat*, December 27, 1895, 6.

180. Ibid.

181. "Green Goods Victim," *Indianapolis Journal*, January 13, 1897, 3.

182. "Farmer Stole Bodies," *Indianapolis Journal*, November 14, 1902, 1.

183. Ibid.

184. Ibid.

185. Ibid.

186. Ibid.

187. "Graves Found Empty," *Indianapolis Journal*, November 15, 1902, 5.

188. "Cantrell Is Rebellious," *Indianapolis Journal*, November 16, 1902, 10.

189. Ibid.

190. "Grand Jury Investigation," *Indianapolis Journal*, November 18, 1902, 3.

191. "Cantrell Before the Grand Jury," *Indianapolis News*, November 18, 1902, 1.

192. "Bookwalter Colored Club," *Indianapolis Journal*, October 3, 1900, 8.

193. "Cantrell's Ready Memory," *Indianapolis Journal*, November 19, 1902, 3.

194. Ibid.

195. "Offer to Cantrell," *Indianapolis Journal*, November 21, 1902, 8.

196. Ibid.

197. "Attempt Made to Have Cantrell Leave Town," *Indianapolis News*, November 20, 1902, 1.

198. Ibid.

199. In the press, his name is generally written as "W.T. Long."

200. "Offer to Cantrell," 8.

201. Ibid.

202. Ibid.

203. "J.M. Bailey Special Judge," *Indianapolis Journal*, November 30, 1902, 8.
204. "Trial of Alexander," *Indianapolis Journal*, November 23, 1902, 10.
205. Ibid.
206. "George Mason Arrested," *Indianapolis Journal*, November 30, 1902, 10.
207. "Trial of Alexander," 10.
208. Central State Hospital.
209. "Trial of Alexander," 10.
210. Ibid.
211. FDR changed Thanksgiving to the third Thursday of November, but for several decades prior, it was held on the last Thursday.
212. "Cantrell Preached to Them," *Indianapolis Journal*, November 28, 1902, 5.
213. Ibid.
214. Ibid. Cantrell later said that the story about the jailhouse sermon on Thanksgiving was false.

Chapter 6

215. "Burden Thrown on the Defense," *Indianapolis News*, December 1, 1902, 1.
216. Ibid.
217. "Trial of Alexander," *Indianapolis Journal*, December 2, 1902, 1.
218. Ibid.
219. Ibid.
220. Ibid.
221. "Defense Scores a Point," *Indianapolis Journal*, December 3, 1902, 10.
222. Ibid.
223. Ibid.
224. "Famine of Cadavers Feared by Physicians," *Indianapolis News*, December 4, 1902, 2.
225. Ibid.
226. Ibid.
227. Ibid.
228. Ibid.
229. Ibid.
230. Ibid.
231. Ibid.
232. "Evidence Against a Hamilton County Man," *Indianapolis News*, December 13, 1902, 20.

233. Ibid.

234. "Farmer Stout Accused," *Indianapolis Journal*, December 14, 1902, 7.

235. "Lucious Stout Lost $31,000," *Indianapolis News*, June 3, 1902, 5.

236. Ibid.

237. "Colored Footracer in Noblesville Court," *Indianapolis News*, February 13, 1903, 11.

238. "People Aroused for a Time," *Indianapolis Journal*, February 13, 1902, 3.

239. "Dr. J.C. Alexander Ill," *Indianapolis Journal*, December 12, 1902, 7.

240. "Dr. Alexander is Sick," *Indianapolis Journal*, December 16, 1902, 8.

241. "Live Man in Coffin," *Indianapolis Journal*, December 30, 1902, 10.

242. Ibid.

243. "Stories of Cantrell and a Physician," *Indianapolis News*, December 30, 1902, 5.

244. Ibid.

Chapter 7

245. "Cantrell Will Stay in Jail," *Indianapolis Journal*, January 4, 1903, 9.

246. Ibid.

247. Ibid.

248. "Rufus Cantrell Changed His Mind," *Indianapolis News*, January 7, 1903, 1.

249. Ibid.

250. "Cantrell Is Sulking," *Indianapolis Journal*, January 8, 1903, 8.

251. Ibid.

252. "Wallace Simms Again," *Indianapolis News*, January 7, 1903, 1 and 11.

253. Ibid.

254. "Ghoulish Work that Was Planned," *Rock Island Argus*, December 26, 1902, 1.

255. "Grave Robbery," *Cincinnati Enquirer*, June 18, 1878, 8.

256. "Human Hyenas," *Cincinnati Enquirer*, May 31, 1878, 8.

257. "Cantrell Is Sulking," 8.

258. "Cantrell Has Moods," *Indianapolis News*, January 8, 1903, 1.

259. Ibid.

260. "Rufus Cantrell Was Before Grand Jury," *Indianapolis News*, January 9, 1903, 10.

261. "Walked Into a Trap," *Indianapolis Journal*, January 5, 1903, 1.

262. Ibid. Just to be sure, Miss Jennie Coffelt's grave was dug up in Franklin, Indiana. Her body was safe and sound. "Miss Coffelt's Grave All Right," *Indianapolis News*, January 7, 1903, 11.

263. Ibid.

264. Ibid.

265. Ibid.

266. Ibid.

267. "Another Alleged Graverobber Caught," *Indianapolis News*, January 5, 1903, 1.

268. Ibid.

269. Ibid.

270. "Result of Scalding," *Indianapolis News*, April 15, 1899, 12.

271. "Walked Into a Trap," 1.

272. "Another Alleged Graverobber Caught," 1.

273. "Another Date Is Fixed," *Indianapolis Journal*, January 7, 1903, 6.

274. "Rufus Cantrell Was Before Grand Jury," *Indianapolis News*, January 9, 1903, 10.

275. "Alleged Grave Robber," *Muncie Evening Press*, January 5, 1903, 2.

276. "Hampton West in Jail, Unable to Furnish Bond," *Hamilton County Democrat*, January 9, 1903, 1.

277. "West Can't Give Bond," *Hamilton County Ledger*, January 9, 1903, 1.

278. Ibid.

279. "West Still in Jail," *Indianapolis News*, January 7, 1903, 1.

280. "Letter Did Not Arrive," *Indianapolis News*, January 20, 1903, 16.

281. "West Sends Pleading Letter to Cantrell," *Indianapolis News*, January 10, 1903, 17.

282. "Long Delayed Letter," *Indianapolis News*, January 31, 1903, 9.

283. "Trial of Dr. Alexander," *Indianapolis News*, January 29, 1903, 1.

284. "Trial of Dr. Alexander," *Indianapolis Journal*, January 6, 1903, 6.

285. "Dr. Alexander's Case Is Again Postponed," *Indianapolis News*, January 6, 1903, 3.

286. "Another Date Is Fixed," 6.

287. "Cantrell Appeals for Aid for the Negroes," *Indianapolis News*, January 23, 1903, 8.

288. "Saws and Files Sent to Rufus Cantrell," *Indianapolis News*, January 20, 1903, 5.

289. Ibid.

290. "Will Get No Aid from the Colored Churches," *Indianapolis News*, January 26, 1903, 12.

291. Ibid.

292. *Indianapolis Recorder*, January 31, 1903, 2.

293. *Indianapolis Recorder*, February 7, 1903, 2.

294. "Long Delayed Letter," 9.

295. "Walked Into a Trap," 1.

Chapter 8

296. "Dr. J.C. Alexander Walks Into Court," *Indianapolis News*, February 2, 1902, 1.

297. Ibid.

298. "Trial of Alexander," *Indianapolis Journal*, February 3, 1903, 1.

299. "Names of the Jurors Who Will Try the Case," *Indianapolis News*, February 4, 1903, 12.

300. Ibid.

301. "Turned Light On Face of His Sweetheart," *Indianapolis News*, February 3, 1903, 10.

302. Ibid.

303. "Jurors Submit to Rigid Examination," *Indianapolis News*, February 3, 1903, 10.

304. Ibid.

305. Ibid.

306. Ibid.

307. Ibid.

308. Ibid.

309. "Jury Now Selected," *Indianapolis Journal*, February 4, 1903, 8.

310. "Defense Is Hit Hard by Court," *Indianapolis News*, February 4, 1903, 1 and 12.

311. Ibid.

312. Ibid.

313. Ibid.

314. Ibid.

315. Ibid.

316. Ibid.

317. "Cantrell on Stage," *Indianapolis Journal*, February 5, 1903, 1 and 6.

318. The following exchange is taken from "Defense Is Hit Hard by Court," 1, 12.

319. Ibid.

320. "Cantrell and Alexander," *Indianapolis News*, February 5, 1903, 3.
321. Ibid.
322. A horse (or horses) that pulled a cart or carriage.
323. "Cantrell's Busy Day," *Indianapolis Journal*, February 6, 1903, 10.
324. Ibid.
325. "Cantrell Grew Funny," *Indianapolis News*, February 5, 1903, 3.
326. Ibid.
327. "Cantrell's Busy Day," 10.
328. Indianapolis newspapers reported that Cantrell was arrested once on October 23, 1900, for a barroom fight and on February 24, 1901, for a fight that involved Cantrell and Garfield Buckner. "Colored Bartender Beaten," *Indianapolis News*, October 23, 1900, 8, and "Three Men Arrested," *Indianapolis Journal*, February 24, 1901, 8.
329. Ibid.
330. "Cantrell on Stage," 1, 6.
331. Ibid.
332. Ibid.
333. Ibid.
334. "Cantrell on Stage," 1, 6.
335. "Cantrell's Busy Day," 10.
336. "State Ends Case," *Indianapolis Journal*, February 7, 1903, 1.
337. Ibid.

Chapter 9

338. "Turn of Defense in Alexander Case," *Indianapolis News*, February 9, 1903, 1, 3.
339. Ibid.
340. Ibid.
341. Ibid.
342. Ibid.
343. "Sanity of Cantrell," *Indianapolis Journal*, February 10, 1903, 10.
344. Ibid.
345. Ibid.
346. "All Evidence Is Now Submitted," *Indianapolis News*, February 10, 1903, 1, 8.
347. Ibid.
348. Ibid.

349. Ibid.

350. Ibid.

351. Ibid.

352. Ibid.

353. "Alexander on Stand," *Indianapolis Journal*, February 11, 1903, 4.

354. "All Evidence Is Now Submitted," 1, 8.

355. "Alexander on Stand," 4.

356. Ibid.

357. "Fate of Alexander," *Indianapolis Journal*, February 12, 1903, 10.

358. Ibid.

359. "Turn of Defense in Alexander Case," 1, 3.

360. "Fate of Alexander," 10.

361. "Attorneys Plead Before the Jury," *Indianapolis News*, February 11, 1903, 1.

362. "Belief that Jury Will Not Agree," *Indianapolis News*, February 12, 1903, 1, 3.

363. Ibid.

364. "Attorneys Plead Before the Jury," 1.

365. "Sheriff Guards Dr. J.C. Alexander," *Indianapolis News*, February 13, 1903, 1, 3.

366. Ibid.

367. "Disagree: And Jury Is Sent Back," *Indianapolis News*, February 14, 1903, 1.

368. He survived.

369. "Jury Discharged," *Indianapolis Journal*, February 16, 1903, 1.

370. "Will Try Him Again," *Indianapolis News*, February 17, 1903, 1.

371. "Control of Dead Bodies," *Indianapolis Journal*, March 9, 1903, 2.

Chapter 10

372. The day before, Judge Alford prevented Cantrell from leaving Indiana to testify in front of a Cook County grand jury after the ghoul was subpoenaed. Alford was clear in his rationale: "I will not allow Cantrell to get beyond the jurisdiction of this court. He can go anywhere in Indiana under the care of a guard, but he can not leave the State. He is wanted here and must stay here." "Keeps Clutch on Cantrell," *Indianapolis News*, March 5, 1903, 8.

373. "Cantrell Was Before Hamilton Grant Jury," *Indianapolis News*, March 7, 1903, 1.

374. Highland Cemetery today.

375. "Cantrell Was Before Hamilton Grand Jury," 1.

376. Ibid.

377. Ibid.

378. "Cantrell in Noblesville," *Indianapolis Journal*, March 7, 1903, 7.

379. "Ghouls Go to Noblesville," *Indianapolis News*, March 11, 1902, 11.

380. "Murder of William Gray," *Indianapolis Journal*, March 15, 1903, 15.

381. Ibid.

382. "Stout Denies Charges," *Indianapolis News*, March 18, 1903, 4.

383. "Will Be Taken to Chicago," *Indianapolis Journal*, March 5, 1903, 8.

384. "Keeps Clutch on Cantrell," *Indianapolis News*, March 5, 1903, 8.

385. "Alexander's New Trial," *Indianapolis Journal*, March 14, 1903, 5.

386. Named in the papers as "Shen Tung."

387. "Shen Tung to Durbin," *Indianapolis Journal*, March 18, 1903, 1, 7.

388. "Simms Gives Details of Doc Lung's Murder," *Indianapolis News*, March 30, 1903, 4.

389. "Sheng Tung to Durbin," *Indianapolis Journal*, March 18, 1903, 1, 7.

390. "Police Discredit Story of Murder," *Indianapolis News*, March 20, 1903, 1.

391. "Are Accused of Doc Lung's Murder," *Indianapolis News*, March 19, 1903, 1, 3.

392. Ibid.

393. Ibid.

394. Ibid.

395. "Little Light on Murder," *Indianapolis Journal*, March 21, 1903, 10.

396. Ibid.

397. "Dead Body Identified," *Indianapolis Journal*, May 23, 1901, 5.

398. "Police Discredit Story of Murder," *Indianapolis News*, March 20, 1903, 1.

399. "Murderers of Doc Lung," *Indianapolis Journal*, March 26, 1903, 1.

400. "Did Cantrell Cause the Arrest of Negroes?," *Indianapolis News*, March 26, 1903, 10.

401. "Doc Lung's Grave Opened," *Indianapolis News*, March 28, 1903, 3.

402 "Police Discredit Story of Murder," *Indianapolis News*, March 20, 1903, 1.

Chapter 11

403. A now gone informal village or hamlet on Indy's west side.

404. "Judge Alford Angry," *Indianapolis Journal*, April 11, 1903, 1.

405. Ibid.

406. Ibid.

407. "Nearly Resulted in a Fist Fight," *Indianapolis News*, April 10, 1903, 1, 4.

408. Ibid.

409. Ibid.

410. Ibid.

411. "Sanity of Cantrell," *Journal*, April 10, 1903, 1.

412. Ibid.

413. "Nearly Resulted in a Fist Fight," 1, 4.

414. "Trial of Alexander Has Been Continued," *Indianapolis News*, April 13, 1903, 11.

415. "Special Judges for Ghoul Trials Chosen," *Indianapolis News*, April 11, 1903, 1.

416. *Polk's Indianapolis City Directory* (Indianapolis, IN: R.L. Polk and Company, 1902), 302.

417. "Special Judges for Ghoul Trials Chosen," *Indianapolis News*, April 11, 1903, 1.

418. "Will Try to Knock Out the Indictment," *Indianapolis News*, April 15, 1903, 3.

419. Ibid.

420. Ibid.

421. Ibid.

422. "Puzzled Over Defense in Graverobbing Case," *Indianapolis News*, April 16, 1903, 3.

423. "M'Cray Makes Charge," *Indianapolis Journal*, April 16, 1903, 7.

424. Ibid.

425. "Connaway Is Accused," *Indianapolis Journal*, April 17, 1903, 1.

426. "M'Cray Makes Charge," 7.

427. Ibid.

428. Ibid.

429. "Puzzled Over Defense in Graverobbing Case," 3.

430. "Connaway Is Accused," 1.

431. Ibid.

432. Ibid.

433. Ibid.

434. "Martin's Fate Now Rests with the Jury," *Indianapolis News*, April 17, 1903, 8.

435. Ibid.

436. Ibid.

437. "Martin Found Guilty," *Indianapolis Journal*, April 18, 1903, 1.

Chapter 12

438. "Cantrell Defended on Plea of Insanity," *Indianapolis News*, April 20, 1903, 12.

439. Ibid.

440. Ibid.

441. Ibid.

442. Ibid.

443 "Cantrell in Court," *Indianapolis Journal*, April 21, 1903, 10.

444. The document also indicated that Cantrell served in Company A of the Twenty-Fourth U.S. Army Infantry Division. He was discharged in 1897 at Fort Douglas, Utah, on a "surgeon's certificate of disability from epilepsy, followed by confusional and suicidal inclinations existing prior to his entry into the United States service." "Prosecution Presents Evidence in Rebuttal," *Indianapolis News*, April 22, 1903, 12.

445. "Cantrell's Sanity Is the Point at Issue," *Indianapolis News*, April 21, 1903, 3.

446. "Prosecution Presents Evidence in Rebuttal," 12.

447. Ibid.

448. Ibid.

449. "Sanity of Cantrell," April 23, 1903, *Indianapolis Journal*, 4.

450. On census records and on her grave marker, she's "Sallie Cantrell."

451. Ibid.

452. "Sanity of Cantrell," April 23, 1903, 4.

453. Ibid.

454. Ibid.

455. Ibid.

456. "Prison for Cantrell," *Indianapolis Journal*, April 24, 1903, 10.

457. Ibid.

458. "Sentence Passed on King of the Ghouls," *Indianapolis New*, April 25, 1903, 23.

459. Ibid.

460. "Rufus Cantrell Found Guilty on Two Counts," *Indianapolis News*, April 24, 1903, 15.

461. Ibid.

462. Ibid.

463. Ibid.

464. "Cantrell to Prison," *News*, April 29, 1903, 3.

465. "Farmers Burned the Men in Effigy," *Indianapolis News*, April 23, 1903, 1.

466. Ibid.
467. Ibid.

Chapter 13

468. "Graverobber Sentenced," *Indianapolis News*, May 7, 1903, 1.
469. Ibid.
470. "More Ghouls Sentenced," *Indianapolis Journal*, May 9, 1903, 7.
471. "Doctors Before Jury," *Indianapolis Journal*, May 12, 1903, 9.
472. Ibid.
473. "Release of the Ghouls," *Indianapolis Journal*, June 28, 1903, 9.
474. "Grave Robbers Given Liberty," *Indianapolis Star*, June 28, 1903, 14.
475. Ibid.
476. "Stout Is Under Arrest," *Hamilton County Ledger*, March 24, 1903, 1.
477. "Stout Will Not Be Tried," *Indianapolis News*, April 2, 1903, 13.
478. "Indiana Happenings," *Indianapolis News*, June 17, 1904, 17.
479. Because of the statute of limitations, the charges against West of stealing Manship's body were also dropped.
480. "Will West Be Tried?," *Hamilton County Ledger*, June 9, 1903, 1.
481. "Long Term of Court," *Muncie Morning Star*, April 18, 1903, 8.
482. "Ghoul's Case Postponed," *Muncie Morning Star*, July 1, 1903, 6.
483. "Rufus Cantrell in Town," *Indianapolis Journal*, July 9, 1903, 1.
484. Ibid.
485. "Graverobber Convicts Brought to This City," *Indianapolis News*, July 9, 1903, 16.
486. "Escape from Hospital," *Indianapolis News*, March 13, 1900, 9.
487. "No Trace Found," *Indianapolis News*, March 19, 1900, 9.
488. Ibid.
489. "Another Weird Story," *Indianapolis Journal*, July 12, 1903, 3.
490. Ibid.
491. "Her Body Not Found," *Indianapolis Journal*, July 14, 1903, 1.
492. "Arrests for Murder," *Indianapolis Journal*, July 15, 1903, 1.
493. Ibid.
494. Ibid.
495. "West Is on Trial," *Hamilton County Ledger*, July 10, 1903, 1.
496. "Jury Impaneled in Hampton West Case," *Indianapolis News*, July 10, 1903, 4.
497. Ibid.

498. Ibid.

499. Ibid.

500. *Hamilton County Ledger*, October 1, 1901, 2.

501. "Jury Impaneled in Hampton West Case," 4.

502. A few witnesses in West's trial implicated Stout in Bracken's theft, although Stout never faced trial for this either. In October 1903, all charges against Stout regarding Bracken were dismissed.

503. "Jury Impaneled in Hampton West Case," 4.

504 Ibid.

505. "Cantrell Testifies Against H. West," *Muncie Morning Star*, July 12, 1903, 11.

506. "Jury Impaneled in Hampton West Case," 4.

507. "West Trial," *Hamilton County Ledger*, July 14, 1903, 1, 4.

508. Ibid.

509. Ibid.

510. "State Has Rested in Hampton West's Case," *Indianapolis News*, July 14, 1903, 1.

511. "West Trial," 1, 4.

512. Ibid.

513. Ibid.

514. "State Has Rested in Hampton West's Case," 1.

515. "West Is Guilty," *Hamilton County Ledger*, July 17, 1903, 1.

516. "Echoes of the West Case," *Hamilton County Ledger*, July 21, 1903, 1.

517. "West as Object of Interest," *Hamilton County Ledger*, July 31, 1903, 8.

518. Ibid.

Chapter 14

519. "Some 'Best Citizens' Probably," *Huntington Herald*, November 2, 1903, 2.

520. "Personal and Social," *Indianapolis News*, September 10, 1903, 7.

521. "Boys Discover Bodies," *Indianapolis Star*, April 12, 1905, 12.

522. Ibid.

523. Eskenazi today.

524. "Dr. W.F. Molt, Physician, Dies in Home," *Indianapolis Star*, January 14, 1958, 8.

525. "New Medical Magazine," *Indianapolis News*, April 18, 1904, 16.

526. "Physician Applies Bitter Epithets," *Indianapolis Star*, May 24, 1905, 14.

527. Ibid.

528. "Adolph Asch, on Police Force 26 Years, Is Dead," *Indianapolis News*, December 29, 1914, 14.

529. "C.A. Manning, Detective, Dies," *Indianapolis Star*, November 5, 1932, 1.

530. Ibid.

531. Ibid.

532. Ibid.

533. Ibid.

534. Ibid.

535. "Dr. Buehler Dies in Texas," *Indianapolis Star*, August 7, 1930, 11.

536. Ibid.

537. "John C. Ruckelshaus, G.O.P. Leader, Dies," *Indianapolis Star*, April 4, 1946, 1.

538. "Cass Connaway Succumbs at 70," *Indianapolis Star*, August 1, 1939, 5.

539. "Taylor E. Groninger, Political Figure, Dies," *Indianapolis News*, July 29, 1958, 7.

540. "Martin M. Hugg, Prominent Attorney, Republican, Succumbs in Home Here," *Indianapolis Star*, October 18, 1938, 4.

541. "Stubbs, Hit by Car, Dies," *Indianapolis Star*, March 4, 1911, 1.

542. "Faculty to Honor Alford at Funeral," *Indianapolis Star*, March 2, 1930, 12.

543. "Services for Charles F. Coffin Will Be Conducted Wednesday," *Indianapolis News*, December 17, 1935, 5.

544. "Two Sets of Charges," *News*, April 3, 1911, 3.

545. "Funeral of Donnell Today," *Indianapolis Star*, October 30, 1906.

546. "City News in Concise Form," *Indianapolis Star*, August 20, 1915, 14.

547. "Yockey Tells Method Used by the Machinists," *Indianapolis News*, November 2, 1916, 9.

548. In the papers, it's called a "blind tiger," a common term for such joints in Indiana.

549. "Eight Tigers Charges Stick," *Indianapolis Star*, November 20, 1918, 8.

550. "Sol Grady, Convicted, Takes Appeal in Case," *Indianapolis News*, May 6, 1919, 27.

551. Ibid.

552. "Cantrell's 'Pal' Insane," *Indianapolis Star*, May 9, 1906, 13.

553. Ibid.

Chapter 15

554. "Rufus Cantrell Makes New Confession to Many Murders," *Indianapolis Star*, August 8, 1903, 1.

555. Ibid.

556. Ibid.

557. Ibid.

558. Ibid.

559. "Dub Him Prince of Liars," *Indianapolis Journal*, August 9, 1903, 10.

560. "Grave Robber Makes Another Confession," *Indianapolis Star*, August 8, 1903.

561. Ibid.

562. "Cantrell, The Ghoul, Will Be Suppressed," *Indianapolis Star*, August 9, 1903, 1.

563. "King of Ghouls Writing a Book," *Indianapolis Star*, July 13, 1903, 1.

564. Goethe Link, "A Bit of Medical History," *Indiana Medical History Quarterly* 3 (December 1977). Article courtesy of the Indiana Historical Society.

565. "They Drove Left," *Indianapolis Journal*, January 5, 1897, 8.

566. "Bookwalter Colored Club," *Indianapolis Journal*, October 3, 1900, 8.

567. "Colored Bartender Beaten," *Indianapolis News*, October 23, 1900, 8.

568. "Three Men Arrested," *Indianapolis Journal*, February 24, 1901, 8.

569. Ibid.

570. "Rumor About Rufus Cantrell," *Indianapolis Journal*, November 11, 1903, 7.

571. *Plymouth Tribune*, June 16, 1904, 5.

572. Ibid.

573. "Rufus Cantrell Not Insane," *Muncie Morning Star*, June 6, 1904, 2.

574. "Parole Again Denied; Cantrell's Third Trial," *Indianapolis Star*, June 3, 1905, 1.

575. Ibid.

576. "Colored Ghoul Is Paroled from Prison," *Fort Wayne Sentinel*, April 30, 1909, 1.

577. Ibid.

578. "Rufus Cantrell Is Married," *Indianapolis News*, December 23, 1909, 2.

579. "Rufus Cantrell Appears in Court," *Indianapolis News*, September 30, 1909, 2.

580. "Rufus Cantrell Is Married," 2.

581. "Ghoul King on Stage," *Muncie Morning Star*, August 16, 1910, 6.

582. "Governor May Stop Ghoul," *Bluefield Evening Leader*, August 18, 1910, 1.

583. "Rufus Cantrell Is Now Preacher," *Muncie Evening Press*, April 30, 1912, 3.

584. Ibid.

585. "'King of the Ghouls' to Stump for Woodrow Wilson," *Indianapolis Star*, September 27, 1912, 12.

586. Ibid.

587. "Colored Men to Line Up Voters for Bell," *Indianapolis News*, October 13, 1913, 1.

588. "Negro Workers Embarrass Bell," *Indianapolis Star*, October 15, 1913, 14.

589. Ibid.

590. "Hallelujah! But It Was a Revel!," *Indianapolis Star*, October 16, 1913, 9.

591. Ibid.

592. "Bookwalter Asserts He Has Won Already," *Indianapolis Star*, October 30, 1913, 7.

593. "Rufus Cantrell Fined $50; to Jail for 30 Days," *Indianapolis News*, February 20, 1914, 1.

594. "Rufus Cantrell Acquitted," *Indianapolis Star*, February 27, 1914, 1.

595. "Colored Democrats Said to Be Against Ed Lyons," *Indianapolis News*, April 14, 1914, 22.

596. "Legal Notice," *Dayton Daily News*, August 11, 1915, 11.

597. "Saloon Case Hearing Is Set for Today," *Indianapolis Star*, November 28, 1915, 12.

598. "Cantrell's Marriage Starts Trouble Anew," *Indianapolis News*, December 24, 1915, 5.

599. Ibid.

600. Ibid.

601. "'King of the Ghouls' and Aid Sentenced," *Muncie Morning Star*, February 6, 1916, 1.

602. "Rufus Cantrell Tells Police of Murder Plot," *News*, December 25, 1915, 1.

603. "Story of Cantrell, Ghoul, Not Verified," *Muncie Morning Star*, December 26, 1915, 1.

604. Sarah "Sallie" Cantrell died in October 1923 and was buried at Crown Hill Cemetery.

605. Cantrell marked "Negro" on the card.

606. "Woman's Skeleton Is Found in Attic," *Indianapolis News*, April 26, 1920, 1, 13.

Epilogue

607. "Says Grave Robbers Are Again at Work," *Indianapolis News*, June 29, 1904, 11.
608. Shultz, *Body Snatching*, 90.
609. Ibid.

ABOUT THE AUTHOR

Chris Flook is a public historian from Muncie, Indiana. He has authored two books in addition to *Indianapolis Graverobbing: A Syndicate of Death*, including *Native Americans of East-Central Indiana* and *Lost Towns of Delaware County*. He also coauthored *Beech Grove Cemetery Comes to Life* in 2016. Since 2017, Flook has written the "ByGone Muncie History" column for the *Star Press*. He works professionally as a motion graphics designer, photographer and documentary filmmaker. He teaches in the Department of Media at Ball State University as a senior lecturer and is an active member of the Delaware County Historical Society.

Visit us at
www.historypress.com